I'M A C

GET ME OUT OF HERE!

I'M A CELEBRITY
GET ME OUT OF HERE!

TREVOR BAKER

GRANADA

First published in Great Britain in 2003
By Granada Media,
an imprint of Andre Deutsch Limited
20 Mortimer Street
London W1T 3JW

I'm A Celebrity Get Me Out Of Here is an
LWT production for ITV

A catalogue record is available from the British Library

ISBN 0 233 00000 3

Jacket design by Sooky Choi with thanks to
Nicky Johnston for his photographs which appear on the back
cover and the top of page 2 of colour section.
With thanks also to Dave Venai for his photograph of
Ant and Dec on the back cover.

Typeset by E-Type, Liverpool

Printed and bound in Great Britain

2 4 6 8 10 9 7 5 3 1

Contents

Introduction

It was almost two years ago this month that a group of bitter TV executives first met for a special meeting in the backroom of a pub in Soho.

After years of watching the growth of celebrity culture, raiding their programme budgets for celebrity expense accounts and celebrity fees, dealing with the insatiable demands of agents and overblown egos, they'd decided that it was about time they had their revenge.

But how? That night, on a few stained beer mats, they scribbled down a scheme so diabolical, so utterly ludicrous, that only in the twisted world of TV would it even have been given the time of day.

They would take those hated celebrities and fly them to the other side of the world – to the most isolated part of the Australian Bush.

There, in a specially prepared camp, they would subject them to a series of humiliations and deprivations: bizarre games, a diet of little more than rice and water, a life without any of the luxuries that they'd come to take for granted, and the constant threat of snakes, leeches, scorpions, ants (and Decs!).

They'd be lured in with the carrot of a million pounds for the charity of their choice – what self-respecting celebrity can be seen to turn down a charity? – and, like so many insects in the jungle, they'd be crushed, utterly destroyed.

With a mocking sense of irony, the execs – by now far gone on fancy cocktails and raw power – christened the programme *I'm A Celebrity ... Get Me Out Of Here!*. It couldn't fail, they laughed, as they stumbled home.

Except that something went wrong. For a start, the cruel execs hadn't realized how popular their series would be. At its peak, more than 12 million people tuned in to watch Tony Blackburn, Rhona Cameron, Nell McAndrew, Christine Hamilton, Uri Geller, Nigel Benn, Tara Palmer-Tompkinson and Darren Day as they struggled to maintain their dignity and composure in the outback.

Even worse, despite the fact that they fought constantly, many of the celebs seemed to come out of it with their reputations enhanced. Christine Hamilton, who'd gone in as the disgraced wife of a disgraced former MP, came out talking about how much 'fun' she'd had.

Tony Blackburn, the eventual winner, said that it changed his life. After years in the wilderness the former Radio One star suddenly found that the general public loved him again – 600,000 of them voted for him in the final reckoning.

A year later he's back on the radio, doing the same catchphrases as he always did, playing the same music, telling the same terrible jokes. The only thing that's changed is that, because of *I'm A Celebrity ...*, he's suddenly a contender again.

So what to do? It would have been easy for the bruised execs to call it a day, but these were the men and women who'd persuaded the British public that *Pets Do the Funniest Things* was a good idea for a series. They were many things but they certainly weren't quitters.

No, they would rebuild *I'm A Celebrity ... Get Me Out Of Here!* bigger, stronger and badder than ever before. They found a new location, an extinct volcano somewhere in the sweltering jungle near Australia's beautiful Gold Coast, and there, surrounded by some of the most dangerous snakes and spiders in the world, they began preparing for Series II and a new batch of unsuspecting celebs.

The Celebrities

LINDA BARKER

Age: 40.
From: Yorkshire.
Occupation: Interior designer, TV presenter and author.
Life story: Linda studied design at art college and became

an interior designer before writing features for women's magazines. In 1994 she made her first TV appearance on the BBC's *Home Front* and the following year she and Laurence Llewelyn Bowen made the pilot for a cheap daytime programme for BBC2 called *Changing Rooms*. Seven years later it's still going, but it's on BBC1 now and it's moved to a peak-time evening spot.

Best known for: Presenting *Changing Rooms*.

Marital status: Married with one daughter.

Before the series started we thought … She'll be the sensible one, getting everyone organized in an understated way while quietly plotting to make over the local trees in bleached pine.

Luxury items: 1. Pillow with pillowcase printed with picture of her husband and daughter. 2. Yoga cards.

Odds: 7/1.

CHRIS BISSON

Age: 27.

From: Manchester.

Occupation: Actor.

Life story: Chris started acting when he was only 13, appearing on *Children's Ward*. Since then he's had all kinds of acting parts, as well as appearing on *RI:SE* and *Soccer AM*. In February 1999 he joined *Coronation Street*, leaving the show earlier this year.

Best known for: Playing Vikram Desai in *Coronation Street* and Saleem in the film *East Is East*.

Marital status: Single.

Luxury items: 1. Inflatable two-seater chair. 2. Supersoaker (water pistol).

Before the series started we thought … Who? Oh, Vikram. The fact that no one knows what the real Chris Bisson is like could be an advantage. He's got to be an improvement on his womanizing, drug-smuggling alter ego Vikram Desai. As long as he doesn't build up huge gambling debts, betray the rest of the celebs, and trick them into trafficking heroin he should be fine.

Odds: 13/2.

JOHN FASHANU

Age: 40.

From: Kensington, London.

Occupation: TV presenter, sports ambassador for Nigeria, owner of the Welsh football club Barrytown.

Life story: John made his debut as a professional footballer for Norwich in 1979, but he's best known for his role as a striker for the marauding Wimbledon side of the mid-eighties. Since then he's enjoyed career highs presenting *Gladiators*, and lows when his estranged gay brother Justin Fashanu committed suicide and when the *Sun* newspaper made unsubstantiated allegations of match fixing against him.

Best known for: Bludgeoning all-comers for Wimbledon and saying 'Awwwooooogaaahhhh!' a lot on *Gladiators*.

Marital status: Married with three children.

Luxury items: 1. Tweezers. 2. Battery-operated electric razor.

Before the series started we thought … He'll want to win. When he was a footballer his nickname was 'Fash the Bash' (rather than, say, 'Fash The Gentle Flower') and even on *Gladiators* you could see he'd have preferred to have been up there on the high beam, battling it out with those padded mallets. Thing is, this time there's no Vinnie Jones to put the squeeze on his competitors. Will he end up trying a bit too hard?

Odds: 8/1.

CATALINA GUIRADO

Age: 24, 28, or 31, depending on whom she's talking to.

From: Spain – moved to London as a child.

Occupation: Model, TV presenter, aspiring singer.

Life story: Catalina seemed to appear from nowhere as the eponymous 'Gorgeous Girl' on Chris Evans's *TFI Friday*. Every week her role was to ask out a self-selecting 'ugly bloke' who would then have the opportunity to reply, 'Sorry, love, you're just not my type.' Yes, it sounds odd, but, hey, that was the nineties. Since then she's made a career as a cover model for innumerable lads' magazines as well as presenting *Single in the City* for Channel 5.

Best known for: Being turned down by ugly blokes every week on *TFI Friday*.

Marital status: Single but linked to Ozzy Osbourne's son Jack Osbourne and anybody else whom the tabloids happen to see within a few feet of her.

Luxury items: 1. Tweezers. 2. Compact (with mirror).

Before the series started we thought … Yeah, but what's she actually famous for? – if you don't fancy her – or *phooargh!* – if you do. Everyone knows that Catalina's there for the delectation of tabloid picture editors, but, if there's a personality behind the face, then she could be on to a winner.

Odds: 10/1.

SIAN LLOYD

Age: 44.

From: Maesteg, South Wales.

Occupation: Weather presenter.

Life story: Sian started out as a researcher for BBC Wales, moved on to S4C, the independent Welsh channel, and she's been ITV's weather presenter for the last nine years, where unsubstantiated rumours of a debauched life behind the clean-cut image have, so far, never quite stuck, despite her nude appearance in the *Daily Mail*.

Best known for: Presenting the weather.

Marital status: In what's described as a 'liberal rela-tionship' with the Lib Dem MP Lembit Opik (the one who's best known for warning us that the planet's about to be wiped out by a rogue meteorite).

Luxury items: 1. Mr Bassey (a cuddly tiger named after Shirley Bassey). 2. 8-Hour Cream

Before the series started we thought … No one's that cheery in real life. Give it a few days and she'll be driven mad by the other contestants demanding to know why she didn't tell them it was going to rain. We expect the real Sian to emerge from that bubbly exterior.

Odds: 9/1.

WAYNE SLEEP

Age: 54.

From: London.

Occupation: Dancer, actor, choreographer and singer.

Life story: Wayne joined the Royal Ballet in 1966 and he was once described as 'the greatest virtuoso produced by the Royal Ballet'. In the seventies and eighties he was one of the few dancers to become a household name.

Best known for: Being Princess Di's favourite dancer.

Marital status: Not the marrying type, although he did once go out with Sarah Brightman. He's now in an on/off relationship with the Spanish dancer Jose Bergera.

Luxury items: 1. Wooden roll-up tap mat. 2. Tap shoes.

Before the series started we thought … Wayne Sleep?

My Gran loves him! Of all the celebrities his skill must be the least useful in the jungle, but, as something of a has-been (sorry, Wayne), is he the new Tony Blackburn, just waiting to revitalize his career with a surprise victory?

Odds: 10/1.

PHIL TUFNELL

Age: Became 37 in the jungle on 29 April
From: East London.
Occupation: TV presenter, cricket pundit.
Life story: Phil Tufnell's nickname 'The Cat' might suggest a lithe, athletic character. In fact it refers to his propensity for falling asleep whenever the opportunity arises. He began playing professional cricket in 1985 and was first picked for England (against Australia – we lost, inevitably) in 1991. As a cricketer he was alternately brilliant and terrible and he finally retired to become a pundit and journalist this year.
Best known for: Taking six wickets for 25 against the West Indies at the Oval in 1991. Being cited in a record-breaking five-person love romp in one of the tabloids and generally being the 'bad boy' of English cricket. Which, admittedly, is rather like being called the 'aesthete of American wrestling' – but even so.
Marital status: Twice married, twice divorced, but in a steady relationship. Two children (one from each marriage).

Luxury item: 1. Pillow. 2. Nothing else.

Before the series started we thought … Britain loves a lovable rogue, and Phil has a quality of not taking things too seriously, which, while it may have been a bit of a disadvantage in the heat of an Ashes Test, could be very useful here.

Odds: 3/1.

DANNIELLA WESTBROOK

Age: 29.

From: Walthamstow, London.

Occupation: Actress.

Life story: Danniella, like half the other young stars on TV, started out at the Sylvia Young Theatre School. At the age of 16 she got a part in *EastEnders*, a pop star boyfriend (Brian Harvey of East 17) and an enormous, £400-a-week coke habit. Since then she's cleaned up and is trying to rebuild her acting career.

Best known for: Playing Sam Mitchell in *EastEnders*. Unprecedented, cocaine-related nose collapse.

Marital status: Married with two children (one from a previous marriage).

Luxury items: 1. Journal (with pictures of her family stuck to it). 2. Pen.

Before the series started we thought … Although she's someone who's in the papers all the time, and had a Channel 4 documentary made about her struggle with drug addiction, we still have very little idea what

Danniella Westbrook is like. After all she's been through (self-inflicted, admittedly), if she's not a complete monster then she's got a strong chance with the sympathy vote.

Odds: 13/2.

ANTONY WORRALL THOMPSON

Age: Became 52 in camp on 1 May

From: Stratford-upon-Avon.

Occupation: Restaurateur and TV presenter.

Life story: Like many of the other celebs, Antony had a proper job for many years, as a chef, and then as the owner of his own chain of restaurants, before he ever showed his face on TV. He started his professional career as a sous-chef and in 1981 he opened his first restaurant, famously serving only starters and puddings. The long-running BBC programme *Food and Drink* then persuaded him to appear, and he's been a panel show regular since.

Best known for: Presenting *Food and Drink* and having a tabloid row with the sinister über-cook Delia Smith.

Marital status: Married to his third wife, former Stringfellows hostess Jacinta. He has two children with her and two with his second wife.

Luxury items: 1. Writing journal. 2. Pen.

Before the series started we thought ... Of all the contestants Antony Worrall Thompson has to be the least popular. For some reason, TV chefs seem to attract inordinate amounts of abuse – especially from each other. Gordon Ramsey memorably described his programme as '*Ready Steady* Twat' and Delia Smith chipped in with 'dreadful, just repulsive'. Just as Jamie Oliver saved his reputation with Fifteen – his restaurant – maybe Anthony can do the same thing with a nicely poached snake. After all, no one can be that unlikable in real life. Can they?

Odds: 12/1.

TOYAH WILLCOX

Age: 44.

From: Birmingham.

Occupation: TV presenter, actress, singer,

Life story: Toyah first came to prominence when she played the part of Mad in Derek Jarman's punk-rock film *Jubilee*. She then had a successful stint as a pop star with huge singles such as 'It's a Mystery' before alternating between appearances on screen, on stage and as a presenter.

Best known for: A successful pop career in the eighties. Presenting various TV programmes, including *Holiday*.

Marital status: Married to the musician Robert Fripp, although at times they've spent as few as 15 weeks a year with each other. No children.

Luxury items: 1. Hot-water bottle. 2. Tweezers.

Before the series started we thought … Will she be able to curtail her industrial-strength flirting? The former presenter

of *The Good Sex Guide* always used to specialize in a body language that the Sirens would have considered a little forward. Since then, though, she's got religion, or at least a wishy-washy spirituality, presenting the *Heaven and Earth Show*. Which is the real Toyah?
Odds: 7/2.

(*All odds from William Hill immediately after contestants were announced.*)

The setting

Everybody liked the setting for last year's *I'm A Celebrity* ... It was beautiful, sunny – kind of nice. In fact, it was a bit too nice. For the second series the producers demanded something a little more, well, demanding.

For weeks they directed their executive helicopters to buzz the jungle, from the sweltering depths of northern Australia to the relatively hospitable national parks in New South Wales. At last they found something. From high up in the sky they spotted a place called Dungay Creek, deep inside a vast, overgrown volcano crater near a small town called Murwillumbah.

It was spectacularly beautiful, with thick tangles of

jungle climbing all the way up from the bubbling creek at the bottom to the steep walls at the top. Even better, they knew that hidden in the Bush all kinds of tantalizing dangers lurked.

The art director and grizzled jungle veteran Ray Pattison was given just a few weeks to transform it into somewhere where the ten celebrities could be completely isolated while a crew of more than 380 people scrambled around them, capturing their every move.

But, before they could begin to create the camp, Ray and his 25-person team had to cut steps painstakingly into the earth, carry four truckloads of equipment up the sloping walls of the volcano and build a ten-metre-high studio.

'There are over a thousand steps,' Ray says, 'and they all had to be cut by hand. All the equipment had to be carried by hand. This is an extremely harsh environment. We saw at least four snakes a day, but maybe we shouldn't tell people that, otherwise they'll say we shouldn't put people down there! But it's gotta be harsh because you don't want it to be a rose garden.

'This was a lot harder than building the set for the first series,' he continued. 'Because it's a rainforest, you don't have strong soil to build on: it's all compost. So a lot of the time we had to dig down through all that.'

Impressive but meaningless facts

For the construction of the camp and the studio Ray and his crew had to order …

- 10 km of timber
- 5,000 square metres of plywood
- 2,000 metal fence pickets
- 10 km of rope
- 200 square metres of foam
- 500 litres of paint
- 10 km of Hessian
- 20 km of fencing wire
- 60,000 litres of water storage
- 6 water pumps
- 52 cubic metres of concrete
- 10 km of black plastic
- 80 tonnes of bush rock
- 5 tonnes of gravel
- 5 tonnes of sand
- 12 snake vivariums (a vivarium is a tank in which snakes are kept)
- 5 beehive cages
- 10 rat cages
- 1 outsized pair of plastic pants

The camp

Until you walk right down into the camp where the celebrities will spend the next 15 days (if they're lucky), it's hard to see how one place can be so isolated and yet available to the scrutiny of millions of viewers 24 hours a day.

Part of it is just geography. Above, if they happen to glance up into the jungle-covered slopes, they may be able to spot one of the hidden cameras, or even one of the walkways where the camera operators and the crew scurry backwards and forwards.

But down in the basin at the bottom their lives are reduced to barely 50 square yards: 10 dusty canvas hammocks; the Bush Telegraph hut (which looks like a dunny); the dunny, which seems to be missing at least two walls; the lower pool, where they go to wash; and the fire, which they'll want to keep fed at all times to ward off mosquitoes and worse.

There are 32 cameras on them at all times, representing not just the crew but millions of people at home, and yet underneath the cool, green fronds of the jungle they'll feel utterly alone.

They can't follow the stream upwards – that way is barred except when they're on the hunt for the celebrity chest – but in the other direction all there is is the Trial

Area, and they won't want to go down there unless they have to. Even half-finished, before the celebs arrive, it looks like a children's playground designed by Cruella DeVille. There's an alarming-looking rope slide strung from one side to another, an unstable-looking bridge (the Bridge of Doom) a sandpit, which apparently will be filled with much more than just sand (the Snake Pit), and, most scarily, a sort of plastic tube that's just big enough for one person to squeeze through (the Rat Run).

Of course, they won't have much choice. The series producers, and the people voting back home, will control almost every aspect of their lives. When the time comes they'll call the celebs, one by one, and tell them which one the public have chosen to take the Bush Tucker trial, or, ultimately, who they've decided should stay and who has to go.

Someone to watch over me

For all its many terrors, the rainforest should be a beautiful place to spend a couple of weeks as long as the celebrities don't think too much about what's lurking in the bushes.

Forget about the creepy-crawlies (for now). The 32

camera positions are staffed by forty different camera operators on rolling shifts, forbidden from communicating with the celebs in any way, watching them silently, continuously, in a menacing uniform of camouflage gear.

And behind them there's another army of camera assistants, caterers, directors, editors, editors' assistants and producers – dozens of producers. You thought producers were big shots? Granada have got 40 of them out here. Disappointingly, none of them seem to smoke cigars or drive around the camp in stretch limos.

That, they leave to the presenters Ant and Dec, who this year of course were joined by former contestant Tara Palmer-Tompkinson, and the journalist Mark Durden-Smith.

Ant and Dec

Is there anyone who doesn't know the history of Ant and Dec? To refresh memories, let's recap. They met on the set of the children's drama *Byker Grove*, became pop stars, released a series of awful but inexplicably successful singles and eventually realized that their talents lay in taking the mickey out of people and somehow not causing offence.

But then, as the Geordie pair are now among the best-known presenters in Britain, you probably already knew that. Just in case anyone's still not sure: Ant is the one on the left of your screen, Dec on your right. They always stand like that.

Ant and Dec arrived in Australia long before the celebrities. They claim that this was in order to take part in a week-long test show with the crew and a cast of actors, but it was noticeable that they spent an awful long time playing football on the beach.

Tara Palmer-Tompkinson

When she appeared on the first series of *Celebrity*, the public perception of TPT was that she was an annoying, spoiled it-girl who'd probably freak out within about a day.

Despite rumours of sex addiction she managed to win over the hearts of the public and eventually finished as runner-up to Tony Blackburn. The turning point was probably when she took a bug shower saying, 'There are people having their legs blown off on the other side of the world. I'm going to do this.'

Her role is very similar to that of ex-footballers on

ITV's *The Premiership* and everyone hopes Tara won't resort to football pundit's phraseology ('Well, you can see what Catalina's done there: she's taken the bug shower early doors, but it looks like Worrall Thompson's looking for some afters').

Mark Durden-Smith

Mark began his career as a proper reporter, doing serious stuff on local radio, and then presenting programmes about rugby for Sky Sports. Since then, though, he's drifted into bad company, anchoring Channel 4's breakfast show *RI:SE* and then *The Wedding Show* for ITV.

It's probably fair to say that he's here because Granada bosses still nervously remembered Tara's appearance on *The Frank Skinner Show* and wanted someone sober and sensible to cut to if things got a little overwrought. Sometimes, after a heavy night, he still dreams of presenting serious news programmes about war and stuff. Probably.

Meanwhile ... back in the UK

The build-up to the first series of *I'm A Celebrity* ... was relatively low-key. There were confident predictions that it would be a terrible failure and that no one would want to watch.

Gradually, though, the country became hooked and the press began playing catch-up to get the dirt on the fall-out between Darren Day and Tara P-T, and the unexpected return of Tony Blackburn as a national icon.

By the time of the second series, they weren't going to get caught out in the same way. The papers were full of speculation about who would be next to brave a couple of weeks in the Bush and there was no shortage of celebs ready to put their names forward.

For a long time everybody knew that Danniella Westbrook was on board, but the list of names to join her changed wildly from day to day. At one point it looked like there was going to be a bizarre John Major cabal out in the jungle with the presence of his ex-mistress Edwina Currie and his former daughter-in-law Emma Noble.

In a parallel universe it would be nice to think there's an *I'm A Celebrity* ... with Edwina and Emma gleefully comparing the relative merits of Major Major and Major Minor.

The surgically expanded model Jordan was also in the frame, but then her name seems to be put forward for everything, be it *Celebrity Big Brother* or documentaries about footballers, plastic surgery and even horse riding.

It was also reported that the show's producers wanted the aristotrash love rat James Hewitt – he'd just been sacked from his job as war correspondent for Fox News – but he wisely realized that the tabloids would eat him alive even before the snakes and spiders got a chance.

Other celebs were only ever contenders in their own desperate sideshow of *I'm A Celebrity ... Kind Of ... Aren't I? ... Let Me Into Here!*.

The irrepressible eighties chef Rustie Lee seemed to think that if she kept asking long enough then eventually studio bosses would relent and let her join the programme – despite the fact that they'd already got a cook in the shape of Antony WT.

Rustie was reported in the papers as saying, 'I'm still hoping they might choose me. I've got a lot to offer. I'll definitely provide a few laughs and I can sing to the other contestants. I'm having my hair done just in case – I'm having it braided.'

She even suggested that she was going to join the programme whether Granada liked it or not. 'I'm going to hire a helicopter and get dropped in,' she claimed. 'It's a fantastic show and I could add so much to it.'

At the same time the *Sun* reported that hundreds of

British backpackers were heading towards the rainforest to try to catch a glimpse of the celebs. One of them declared, rather optimistically, that anyone who got into the celebs' camp would be 'a real star'.

Meanwhile, the first sign of spats to come came with a mischievous interview with Phil Tufnell, in which he put the boot into Catalina. In its own pithy style the *Sun* reported, 'Fur is set to fly when The Cat comes face-to-face with The Wild Cat in the jungle.' It goes on to report Phil as saying, 'I met her at a Granada preview and I already know she's not my type. I like women who behave like women – a bit of dignity, a bit of fun and a lot of brains up top.'

'I will have nothing in common with Phil Tufnell,' Catalina is reported to have retorted. 'I like men with a bit of sophistication, a bit of class. I don't like men who think they are God's gift because they can do something with a ball – usually it's because they can't do it with their own balls.'

The *Sun* Journalist Frank Thorne then tried to steal a march on his rivals by hacking his way into the camp. In the classic tradition of tabloid journalism, he had a quick look at the bug-infested jungle, then made his excuses and left.

And, for a reminder that celebs are (allegedly) real people, there was a report that Danniella Westbrook's husband Kevin Jenkins wouldn't be watching the programme. 'I can't bear to see her cry,' he told the *Sun*. 'It would just break my heart.' Ahhhh.

Five entirely gratuitous Catalina stories in the build-up

1 **Seven days to go**: Cat fight – Phil Tufnell disses Catalina.
Source: *Sun*.
Headline: 'I won't be getting jiggy in the jungle … I've had more than enough of women like Catalina'.
Key quote: 'I don't like men who think they are God's gift because they can do something with a ball – usually it's because they can't do it with their own balls.'
Picture: A cricket bat. And Catalina in a bikini.

2 **Five days to go**: Cat says she wants sex in the jungle
Source: *Sun*.
Headline: 'I don't do married men, or women … that just leaves *Corrie* star Chris'.
Key quote: 'I don't have a problem with sex – I have a problem with not having sex. I haven't had a romp since February and that was only a brief fling. I enjoy sex but I don't do married men and I don't do women.'
Picture: Cat reclining, wearing a bikini, looking sultry but sophisticated.

3 Four days to go: Cat says she's had sex on a beach
Source: *News of the World*.
Headline: 'I'm a celebrity and I love having sex in the open air'.
Key quote: 'I didn't want to do it in the sand 'cos that gets in all the wrong places. So we went to the rocks.'
Picture: Cat standing, wearing a bikini, with bared teeth.

4 Two days to go: Cat says she's going to quit because it's raining
Source: *Sun*.
Headline: 'Rain? Get me outta here!'
Key quote: 'I'm not good in the rain. If it keeps going on like this I'm going to have to walk! I wanted to get a tan in the next couple of days so I'd look gorgeous in the jungle but this is a total washout.'
Picture: Cat lying on the floor, growling, looking mucky.

5 One day to go: Cat thinks her bottom is too big
Source: *Sun*.
Headline: 'Cat: I want a new bot'.
Key quote: 'I hate my bum – it's too big and I'm worried about showing it off. There's no way I'll wear a thong in the jungle.'
Picture: Cat standing side on to the camera, wearing pale-yellow bikini, looking melancholy (owing to substandard bottom).

The celebs arrive

As they step off the plane and into the blinding sunlight of Australia's beautiful Gold Coast, the celebrities will probably breathe a big sigh of relief and inwardly decide not to sack their agents after all.

The Gold Coast is to the southern cities of Sydney and Melbourne what Australia itself is to the UK. It's a sunnier, happier place, where the surf is high and inhibitions are low. Throughout the year sun-seekers flock here in search of a good time or to escape from what passes for winter in the south.

What with travelling first class and arriving at one of the most luxurious hotels in the country, the celebs hardly need to feel that they've left the Met Bar (if the Met Bar was a two-minute walk from surf-kissed beaches and full of bronzed gods and goddesses, rather than just Dean Gaffney and his mates). The temperature is typically about 25 degrees Celsius, and there's usually several hours of sunlight every day.

Of course *I'm A Celebrity … Get Me Out Of Here!* isn't *Ibiza: Uncovered*. When the time comes the celebrities are to be whisked by helicopter into the dense rainforest a few miles west – and there's a reason why they don't call it the 'pleasantsunshineforest'.

A couple of months before the British series, the

American version of *Celebrity* ... checked into Dungay Creek and it rained almost solidly for the whole two weeks. The eventual winner, Cris Judd, almost started to wish he was back with his ex-wife J-Lo. (But only almost.)

But the celebs' first taste of the jungle comes later. Before that, even before they've had a chance to recover from their jetlag, they're ushered into a makeshift classroom to meet a genial, white-haired medic called Bob McCarron and a rugged ex-stuntman called John Walton.

From the lowliest runner to the series producer, everybody has to go through their spine-chilling lecture about the dangers lurking in the Bush. This means not just the snakes, spiders, leeches and scorpions, but also floods, lightning, falling logs and hostile terrain. Who knew that Mother Nature had quite so many varied and ingenious ways of killing you?

And even the Chamber of Horrors would probably reject Bob's props as a little too gruesome. He has a large wooden box stuffed with petrified funnel-web spiders, wasps and huge ants plus a couple of very-much-alive leeches and even a wriggling, hissing rough-scaled snake – one of the most dangerous snakes in the world.

'Look at that one,' Bob laughs a little too heartily, pointing to a huge, brightly coloured wasp. 'That's straight out of Disney!'

No, Bob, Disney's insects are nice, friendly creatures who buzz around happily, passing on useful information to the Seven Dwarfs. These wasps look as if they'll fly off with your picnic basket, down a pot of jam in one greedy slurp and spit the pips right back in your face.

And look at the spiders. Even if you didn't know that the funnel-web spider is, quite simply, the most dangerous spider on earth, you wouldn't want to mess with it. It's huge, fat and ugly – the bouncer of the arachnid world with a fat, bulging belly and a belligerent, 'you lookin' at me?' expression.

Luckily, Bob has plenty of words of reassurance for the celebrities. Unfortunately, he has even more words to scare them senseless and make them wish they'd never left Hampstead.

The terrifying wisdom of Bob

SPIDERS

There are more than forty varieties of spider located around the camp, and all of them are venomous. The worst of these are the funnel-web spider and the famous red-back spider (a close relative of the better-known black widow).

When disturbed, funnel-web spiders rear up like

startled horses, their enormous fangs literally dripping with poison.

The celebs also have to look out for tarantulas – Australia's are the most aggressive in the world – and white-tailed spiders, who make up for their relative anonymity with a terrifying, flesh-rotting bite. Their poison is described as 'necrotic', which means it spreads through the flesh around the area of the bite, increasing the damage by killing cells.

Victims also claim that the symptoms reappear every six months or every year after the attack occurs. The fact that white-tailed spiders have yet to appear in a Hollywood movie, or even a *When Spiders Get Mad* documentary, can only mean that they need to get a better agent.

Bob's bad news: 'This area is notorious for funnel-web spiders. They are the most dangerous spider in the whole world. You might also see bird-eating spiders – they're about the size of guinea pigs.'

And the good news: 'No one has died of a funnel-web-spider bite in the last seventeen years since the antivenom was introduced. When you're asleep there'll be spiders but they'll crawl over you and you won't even know they're there.' (Bob seemed to think this was good news.)

LEECHES

Leeches love the damp conditions of the rainforest. They hang around in trees, lurk in bushes and swim through shallow water, just waiting for some unsuspecting celebrity to pass.

They latch on to your skin with one end while injecting an anaesthetic with the other so that you don't notice that they're sucking your blood. Rather like the free drinks they hand out at press launches.

Bob's bad news: 'We've treated ninety-nine per cent of the crew for leeches. You'll go to scratch your foot and your whole sock will be covered in blood. One of the girls even got bitten down the bikini line by a leech.'

And the good news: 'You can get rid of them just by sprinkling a little bit of salt on their backs. They'll curl up and drop off.

SCORPIONS

Dungay Creek is crawling with scorpions.
Bob's bad news: 'The scorpions round here will give you a nasty sting, a bit like a bee.'

And the good news: 'They're not dangerous.'

SNAKES

This area of New South Wales is home to 14 different snakes, including the lethal taipan, and 12 of them are venomous. Most of them are nondescript-looking creatures who blend in with the logs and the undergrowth, but the biggest of them, the carpet python, can grow up to 2.5 metres long and kill a grown man with its crushing grip.

Bob's bad news: 'The worst thing that we've had to treat anyone for is snakebite – someone got bitten by a rough-scaled snake. Rough-scaled snakes are the sixth most venomous and the second most aggressive snakes in the world. They carry enough poison to kill a hundred and forty fully grown men in a row.'

And the good news: 'They very rarely release their poison when they bite defensively.'

TICKS

Along with leeches, ticks are one of the more ubiquitous hazards the celebs have to face. The little parasites lurk in the bushes waiting to dig their way into anyone walking past (which should remind Danniella of the paparazzi when she was going through her one-barrelled-nose period).

There are several species, but the most dangerous is the evocatively named paralysis tick. They burrow under the skin and secrete a poison from their saliva that causes a slow, and in rare cases fatal, paralysis.

If found in time, they shouldn't be a problem, and Bob advises the celebrities to check each other carefully, which at least will help them to get to know each other better.

Bob's bad news: 'A lot of people think you can get ticks out by burning them with a cigarette. Don't do that: you'll do more damage by burning yourself.'

And the good news: 'With a pair of tweezers they're usually fairly easy to pull out, and we can do that for you.'

MOSQUITOES

In the history of humanity, mosquitoes, with a little help from their chum malaria, have killed far more people than any other creature on the planet put together. Luckily, Australia's mozzies don't carry malaria, but they're still not particularly nice.

Bob's bad news: 'One mosquito in a hundred carries moss river fever, which puts you in hospital for a week.'

And the good news: 'Everybody's been bitten by mosquitoes and nobody's had it yet.'

Welcome to the jungle

After they've had their lecture from Bob McCarron and John Walton, all that awaits is for the celebs to collect their jungle gear – and then their helicopter awaits. First, though, they need to know the rules. This is a verbatim copy of the top-secret document that the celebs received ...

THE RULES

Object of the show:
The object of the show is simple: during the first week one of you will be chosen each day, by the viewers back in the UK, to undertake a 'Bush Tucker Trial'. The object of the Trial is to win food for the group. In the second week the British public will be voting to decide who stays in camp. The winner is the last to leave the jungle.

You are living in a potentially lethal environment. Most of the programme rules are in place to help us ensure your safety and you will be expected to abide by them.

The key rules are:

THE MAP YOU HAVE BEEN PROVIDED WITH INDICATES THE BOUNDARIES OF CAMP IN RED. TO ENSURE YOUR SAFETY YOUR MOVEMENTS OUTSIDE THESE BOUNDARIES WILL BE RESTRICTED.

THERE MUST ALWAYS BE FIVE PEOPLE IN CAMP AND NO-ONE SHOULD EVER LEAVE THE CAMP ALONE.

YOU ARE FORBIDDEN FROM LEAVING CAMP VIA THE UPSTREAM EXIT EXCEPT DURING THE HUNT FOR A CELEBRITY CHEST.

THE ONLY AREA OUTSIDE CAMP THAT YOU HAVE ACCESS TO AFTER DARK IS THE LOWER POOL. HOWEVER, THIS IS RESTRICTED TO TWO PEOPLE AT ANY ONE TIME. UNLESS AT THE LOWER POOL, NO-ONE IS TO LEAVE CAMP AFTER DARK.

WHENEVER YOU LEAVE CAMP A FILM CREW MUST ACCOMPANY YOU. THEY HAVE BEEN TRAINED IN THE LOCAL AREA AND WILL ALSO BE ABLE TO GET HELP TO YOU QUICKLY IF YOU WERE TO COME TO ANY HARM. IF THE PRODUCER TELLS YOU THAT AN AREA IS OUT OF BOUNDS IT IS PROBABLY FOR YOUR SAFETY AND YOU MUST NOT PERSIST IN FOLLOWING THAT ROUTE.

ALL BRIDGES ARE OUT OF BOUNDS. EACH DAY ONE CELEBRITY WILL BE INFORMED THAT THEY ARE TO DO A BUSH TUCKER TRIAL. UP TO FOUR OTHER CELEBRITIES MAY ACCOMPANY THEM TO THE FOOT OF THE TRIALS BRIDGE BUT ONLY THE CHOSEN CELEBRITY MAY CROSS THE TRIAL BRIDGE. THE PATH TO THE TRIALS AREA IS OUT OF BOUNDS AT ALL OTHER TIMES.

YOU WILL BE INFORMED IMMEDIATELY PRIOR TO THE LIVE SHOW GOING TO AIR. DURING THIS TIME ALL CELEBRITIES MUST REMAIN IN CAMP. AT SOME POINT DURING THE BROADCAST YOU WILL BE INSTRUCTED TO TAKE YOUR SEATS AROUND THE FIRE.

IF YOU NEED TO COMMUNICATE WITH PRODUCTION YOU MAY DO SO VIA THE BUSH TELEGRAPH (INDICATED ON YOUR MAP).

YOU MUST WEAR YOUR RADIO MICROPHONES AT ALL TIMES AND CHANGE THE BATTERIES WHEN REQUESTED TO DO SO. THE LOOP OF THE MICROPHONE LEAD THAT GOES AROUND YOUR NECK MUST ALWAYS BE WORN ON THE OUTSIDE OF YOUR CLOTHING. DON'T WORRY IF IT IS RAINING THEY ARE WATERPROOF.

YOU MUST ALWAYS KEEP THE CAMP FIRE BURNING BUT NEVER LET IT GET OUT OF CONTROL.

YOU ARE LIVING WITHIN A VERY DELICATE ECOSYSTEM AND DURING YOUR STAY YOU MUST ENDEAVOUR TO PROTECT IT. PLEASE NOTE THAT WITHIN CAMP THERE IS ONE PARTICULARLY RARE TREE (WE HAVE INDICATED THIS ON YOUR MAP) PLEASE DON'T ALLOW IT TO BE HARMED IN ANY WAY

SMOKERS WILL BE GIVEN A RATIONED SUPPLY EACH DAY. IN ADDITION TO THE HARM IT COULD DO TO THE ECOSYSTEM, WE CANNOT STRESS TO YOU STRONGLY ENOUGH HOW DANGEROUS A MISPLACED LIT CIGARETTE CAN BE.

WHEN THE FOREST IS DRY THE RISK OF BUSH FIRES IS EXTREMELY HIGH. ALL SMOKERS MUST DISPOSE OF THEIR CIGARETTES IN THE CAMP FIRE. IF YOU AREN'T NEAR THE FIRE YOU SHOULD STUB YOUR CIGARETTE OUT ON A ROCK & POCKET THE STUB UNTIL YOU CAN PUT IT IN THE FIRE LATER. NEVER DROP THEM IN THE JUNGLE!

YOU WILL BE PROVIDED WITH RATIONS OF RICE AND BEANS. THE CONTAINER IN WHICH THEY ARE SUPPLIED WILL INDICATE HOW LONG THE RATIONS SHOULD LAST.

ADDITIONAL FOOD CAN BE EARNED THROUGH THE BUSH TUCKER TRIAL. YOU MUST NEVER ATTEMPT TO EAT ANY BUSH FOOD UNLESS THE PRODUCTION TEAM GIVES IT TO YOU – MUCH OF IT IS EXTREMELY POISONOUS. AUSTRALIAN LAW PROTECTS ALL WILDLIFE, INCLUDING THE FISH LIFE WITHIN THE CREEK THAT SURROUNDS YOU. YOU MUST NOT KILL IT OR EAT IT. THERE ARE SOME FRESHWATER CRAYFISH IN THE CREEKS. YOU ARE FREE TO CATCH AND EAT THESE.

YOU SHOULD WASH AT THE LOWER POOL SITUATED DOWNSTREAM OF CAMP. ALL POTS AND PANS SHOULD BE

WASHED DOWNSTREAM OF THIS POOL TO AVOID YOU
WASHING IN DIRTY WATER.

THERE IS A WATER CONTAINER IN CAMP. THIS IS WHERE
YOU SHOULD STORE YOUR DRINKING WATER. YOU SHOULD
COLLECT WATER TO FILL THIS CONTAINER FROM THE CREEK
JUST ABOVE THE LOWER POOL, WHERE THE WATER IS FAST
FLOWING. ALL WATER MUST BE BOILED BEFORE IT IS
PLACED IN THE CONTAINER OR DRUNK. THERE IS A
SEPARATE CONTAINER IN THE TOILET AREA FOR WASHING
HANDS. THERE IS NO NEED TO BOIL THE WATER YOU PUT IN
HERE.

YOU MUST DRINK A MINIMUM OF FOUR CANTEENS OF
WATER A DAY. IF IT IS HOT, OR YOU HAVE HAD ALCOHOL,
YOU SHOULD DRINK A MINIMUM OF EIGHT.

YOU MAY REQUEST TO SEE DR SANDRA SCOTT, THE
PRODUCTION'S PSYCHIATRIST, AT ANY TIME. SHE WILL
COMMUNICATE TO YOU INDIVIDUALLY THE RULES
ASSOCIATED WITH HER CONSULTATION.

YOU WILL FIND A BASIC FIRST AID KIT IN CAMP FOR THE
TREATMENT OF MINOR AILMENTS. THIS KIT ALSO INCLUDES
GUIDELINES THAT INFORM YOU OF WHAT YOU SHOULD
TREAT YOURSELF AND THOSE CONDITIONS THAT REQUIRE
HELP. FOR MORE SERIOUS CONDITIONS YOU SHOULD
REQUEST A CONSULTATION WITH THE PRODUCTION'S MEDIC
THROUGH THE BUSH TELEGRAPH.

AS AND WHEN NEW ELEMENTS ARE INTRODUCED INTO THE
PROGRAMME THE PRODUCTION TEAM WILL COMMUNICATE
ANY RULES ASSOCIATED WITH THEM.

APART FROM THE PRODUCERS, NONE OF THE CREW IS

PERMITTED TO COMMUNICATE WITH YOU IN ANY WAY.
PLEASE DON'T TAKE OFFENCE OR PUT THEM IN AN
UNCOMFORTABLE POSITION BY TRYING TO COMMUNICATE
WITH THEM.

Sounds pretty nasty, doesn't it? But, then, that's the point.

Ready To Go In

God, it seems, hates celebrities. When they arrived on the Gold Coast, it was bathed in sunshine, but in the meantime the heavens have opened, roads near Dungay Creek have flooded and the camp is very wet indeed.

At one point there's even a suggestion that the celebs might have to abandon the helicopter and arrive by barge. At the hotel for their final training session, though, they're already getting into the habit of putting a brave face on things – in some cases with more success than others.

Phil seems to have done it with the aid of a drink or two – but, then again, his air of rosy bemusement is such a part of his personality that artificial stimulants may not be as crucial as you'd think.

Even when a python wraps itself around his neck at the photocall, he just looks like somebody trying to remember who bought him this weird tie for Christmas – until, that is, the snake defecates messily all over him.

You just don't bump into snakes on Sutton High Street, he observes correctly.

Elsewhere, the jolly-hockey-sticks award for Being Practical and just generally Getting On With It is already under way.

Linda Barker is probably the winner so far, but Antony WT manages to look at Bob's dead spiders with the indulgent air of someone who's cooked and eaten much worse. Danniella, you imagine, has snorted worse; Toyah is clearly telling herself that karma (or some celestial spirit with too much time on its hands) will take care of her; and Sian Lloyd seems to be floating away somewhere in her own little world of fluffy clouds and tigers named after Shirley Bassey.

That just leaves John and Catalina to look genuinely nervous, although in Cat's case there's an element of scream-queen pouting in the Penelope Pitstop style: Rescue me, boys, the nasty spiders are *sooo* scary ...

Medic Bob McCarron was highly impressed by the whole group, though. They were a hundred per cent better than the Americans, he said. They didn't come out here with the attitude that they could have anything they wanted. They were all putting on their jungle gear straightaway because they knew that that was right for the jungle. The Americans wanted something a bit more designer!

Nevertheless he had a warning that there were harder times to come: By the fourth day – when they're tired and they're hungry – that's when the bickering starts, he predicted.

> **Bob's pick to win**: Toyah. I hope she wins. She's gutsy and wide-eyed. She's come here to learn something and she seems very open.
>
> **To leave first**? I think Linda could go first: she seems to be lacking the spark that some of the others have got.

Of course, in the murky world of celebritydom, Getting On With It also means Getting Away With It. The producers expected a few of the celebs to try to smuggle in a few extra luxuries, but they almost got away with a clever double-bluff.

An initial search of their bags and clothes turned over a huge and blatant haul: a razor, pens, tomato ketchup, a torch (Antony), a comb, make-up, mouth freshener, lip balm, extra cigarettes, a cigarette lighter, a potato peeler, plasters (Wayne), incense (Linda), a fishing net (which Fash had hidden in his pants), crisps and chocolate (Phil) tweezers, a pair of posh slippers (Antony). How did they think they'd get away with all that?

The answer is, they probably didn't. When they got into the camp, it was discovered that they'd got even more contraband: Catalina had cleverly worn her hair up and had cigarettes concealed inside; Fash was also later forced to hand over two pairs of black knickers, which were assumed to be Cat's (not *The* Cat's – that would be too bizarre); Antony had smuggled some spices in, strapped to his ample stomach; and Danniella had somehow smuggled in a watch.

We saw her sitting by the lower pool, one of the producers said. She was chewing gum, which she's allowed, apparently, because it's Nicorette gum. She was reading a book, which she *was* allowed because it was something to do with her addiction programme, and she was wearing a watch! It was just like she was on holiday.

There were also whispers around the production team that Cat had gone into the toilet with Toyah to try to persuade her to hide some more cigarettes in her hair, too. Unfortunately the reformed punk wasn't interested. Bitch wouldn't do it, Cat supposedly laughed when she came out.

Of course, before all that, the celebs had the small matter of a two-and-a-half-hour hike to the camp from the helicopter drop. If they'd been alone we'd probably still be looking for them today, but they were guided by the legendary Bush Tucker man Steve 'Bush Dog' McGrath.

'I first met them the day before when we were teaching them survival skills,' he explains. 'It was still pretty exciting. They were learning a lot and it was still a game to start with, but then the realism set in.

'They were paying attention, though,' Steve admits. 'A lot of people think, Oh, our manager or whatever has got us to do this. We don't need to worry about anything. They wouldn't let anything happen to us. They can't afford to lose us! But they weren't like that. By the time they got to the landing spot their eyes were sticking out like Coke bottles. They were genuinely concerned about what they were getting into. We'd had a shitload of rain the night before, so it was really wet down there. I took fifteen leeches off me during the walk.'

The celebs were even more alarmed when their bearded guide said he'd have to leave them to make the last of the journey on their own. 'Keep to the path!' he told them in true horror-movie fashion before disappearing, but in this case the 'path' looked suspiciously like a river.

Like Bob, though, Steve was generally very impressed by the celebrities' attitude. 'I'd never heard of any of them,' he says. 'I don't follow celebrities or sport or anything like that but I found them all very nice people. It was a disappointment that I couldn't go into the camp with them.'

The Long March

Footage of the walk wasn't shown on TV but here is Steve 'Bush Dog' McGrath's guide to how our ten heroes comported themselves on the two-and-a-half hour trek to camp.

WAYNE SLEEP

'The person who springs to mind first is Wayne. What a laugh! You need someone like that. He just took the piss out of himself and everyone really liked him. He wanted to bring this tap mat into the camp but it's just because he realized that people needed to be entertained.'

SIAN LLOYD

'I imagine she looks more at home presenting the weather than she does out in the rainforest. She's a very pretty girl.'

DANNIELLA WESTBROOK

'If anyone gets into trouble, I'd imagine it'd be Danni. I hear she's had problems in the past and she was getting pretty distraught on the walk down because I couldn't tell them where they were or how far away from the camp they were. She was saying, "I really need to know when we're going to get there, Bush Dog."'

CATALINA GUIRADO

'Catalina really toughened up. They all did during the walk. She got caught in some lawyer vine – that's one of the things that you don't want to grab hold of in the jungle – and she was really tangled in it. That freaked her out pretty bad but she got over it.'

ANTONY WORRALL THOMPSON

'Antony will give them all the shits. [He doesn't mean literally through his cooking, but figuratively through his personality.] He was very keen to be demanding and commanding. I wouldn't want to be left alone in the jungle with him!'

JOHN FASHANU

'John told me within five minutes of meeting him that he couldn't stand snakes and insects and he hated the Bush, but I think they chose wisely electing him leader on the first day. He's the biggest and strongest of them and I think he'll get over his phobias.'

PHIL TUFNELL

'Phil was a laugh. The old cod-rubber I called him! He was always rubbing his cods! [The cods are the area that cricketers always seem to be polishing their cricket balls against.] I said to him, "You've got to be the cricketer!" He's got a great sense of humour.'

CHRIS BISSON

'Chris was the most laid back. He was just getting the hang of it. In a group like that you need to be pretty loud to get attention, and maybe he's a bit too quiet, but he's got a sense of humour, too. He brought a water pistol with him, which is probably good, because boredom's the worst thing they'll have to deal with.'

TOYAH WILLCOX

'I liked Toyah. She kept on saying how wonderful everything was. I told her, "That's good. You've got to make it into a positive thing. The glass is half full, rather than half empty." She was up for trying things, sliding on her bum down the hill and things like that.'

LINDA BARKER

'She was pretty happy to go with the flow. She didn't come across as a leader, or as someone who'd hold everybody back. She wasn't grumpy or anything like that.'

Steve's pick to win: 'The tip in London is Phil, isn't it? I'd like to see one of the girls win – maybe the weathergirl.'

To leave first? 'I wouldn't be surprised if Danni votes herself out! From what I've seen so far, I think they'll want to get Antony out. I think he'll destroy the morale of the group by being too domineering.'

Day One

When they reach the camp the jolly holiday spirit comes back stronger than ever. Don't these people know they're supposed to be going through celebrity hell?

To begin with, it doesn't seem so. They quickly elect Fash to be their leader, and seem happy to follow his orders. Antony reveals that he's managed to smuggle in some spices (the celebs all exclaim, 'Spices!' in an enthusiastic manner, while inwardly thinking, Spices? Bloody chef!) and, endearingly, they're soon naming bits of the camp after their forbears: Uri's point, the Tony Blackburn walkway and the Tara Hop Road.

From then on it becomes a competition to see who can get their 'specialist skill' into play first. It's like one of those superhero cartoon stories in which they all get to use their power once in each episode, except that here, instead of shooting fire or ice out of their fingers, they're left with modelling, spin bowling, tap dancing …

Antony, of course, has got a big advantage as someone with a more universal skill, and he's soon inspecting the kitchen utensils. 'Pretty primitive cooking pans, aren't they?' he opines breezily, before taking charge of the rice and beans. That's one-nil to Antony WT, it seems.

Implausibly, though, Catalina is the next to remind everyone what she's famous for with an impromptu lesson for the other celebs in how to walk down a catwalk, looking like a million dollars even in the pouring rain and playing her unique selling point for all it's worth.

Sian tries to keep up, but her comment that 'there's a bit of blue sky up there' just seems to show up the essential ridiculousness of the fact that she gets paid good money to say pretty much the same thing in her day job – drawing good-humoured, but faintly mocking shouts of 'Go, weather girl!' from the other celebs.

Wayne is playing the long game and he doesn't get his tap mat out until later in the evening, when the novelty of the camp has worn off and they're looking for some entertainment. His secret weapon, to persuade the others to join in, is an implausible story about how Phil Tufnell is surprisingly good at tap dancing.

Phil, for his part, resists the temptation to teach the other celebs to throw a googly, but then he's got his new career, too – that of lovable rogue – and at that he's working expertly.

So far, Linda, Chris, Danniella and Toyah are keeping a relatively low profile, but if the day has a winner it has to be Fash. Somehow he's managed to expand his two specialist skills, those of Football Star and *Gladiators* presenter, into the broader role of Action Hero, and at times he seems to inspire genuine hero worship among the other celebs – particularly after he earns them seven meals as the first one of them to undertake a Bush Tucker Trial.

See the mighty Fash defeat his fear of heights over the Bridge of Doom! See him make pouring a gallon or so of maggots into plastic pants look like a bad day on the bridge over the River Kwai!

The most impressive part of it is that, despite the fact that Fash seems to have more phobias than any of them – snakes, spiders, heights – he makes his struggle to deal with them look like a kind of heroism.

And the other celebs do seem genuinely to appreciate his leadership, especially when he encourages them to form a massage conga. If Day One is all about the ten of them bonding into a seemingly insoluble unit, then this is the moment when they really squish into a touchy-feely, lovey-dovey, happy-camper mass.

Unfortunately, those of us who have evil thoughts about something bad happening to make things more exciting are made to regret them very quickly.

It's shortly after the heavens have opened again, and they're pulling on their see-through rain macs (glorified plastic bags). Toyah is smiling approvingly. 'We're gonna be warm in these,' she coos. 'These are good.'

They should know that God doesn't like that kind of thing – hapless mortals mocking his powers with little more than a Tesco bag with armholes. And for once we're talking about the 'real' God – not just the chortling producers sitting in their mobile offices higher up the volcano.

His revenge, or at least a warning shot, comes quickly. Antony is standing by his half-finished bed when there's a mighty crash and an enormous clod of plant life, mud and branch hurtles from the treetops above, only just missing his head and brushing his arm.

The sense of shock is genuine. Maybe it wouldn't have killed him but it would have certainly hurt, and it's touching how quickly the other celebs rally around, with Danniella and Wayne picking bits of mud out of his clothes and hair.

Antony was hot favourite to be the most hated of the celebs to start with, so if they can do that for him they must be getting on well. Is it possible that, so far, they actually like each other?

And that's not the only brush with tragedy (or at least tragicomedy) that they've been faced with. It's an unfortunate tribute to Chris's inability to make any kind of impression at all so far that he almost knocks himself out trying to 'save' Catalina from one of those scary spiders; and yet most people here, let alone in the UK, still keep forgetting that he's in the show.

Maybe it's because he reacts as though the spider had just exploded when he hits it – flying backwards in a comic fashion. Only later, when you find out that he had to go and see the doctor, do you feel mildly guilty for laughing.

Still, it's just another thing to make the celebs realize that the jungle can be a dangerous place and the danger seems to have brought them closer together. On the first day, most of the celebs, even Antony, actually seemed quite nice.

Can it last, though? Around the production offices there are various people who are experts in Bush survival, and various people who are experts in reality TV, and they all agree on one thing: by the third day the first celebs will begin to crack.

Quote of the day

Wayne (putting on his damp rain mac):
'I feel like a used condom!'

Day Two

Third day, did they say? Reality-show inflation has obviously set in since last time, because there are already signs of severe stress among our heroes. Even at home people are starting to show the strain. Apparently half the Middlesex cricket team had to be treated for shock after witnessing Phil Tufnell turn down a free drink.

More of that later, though. The first item on today's agenda is the passing of the leadership baton. As ever, Fabulous Fash makes the relatively simple proceedings sound like a cross between the Gettysburg Address and a find-your-inner-hero motivational video.

'I'm giving it to Phil,' he explains nobly, 'because it's his birthday, and I've found that the extra responsibility of being leader often makes the jester buckle down.' To his credit, Phil actually looks quite touched by this gesture and he does his best to look like a mature, responsible 37-year old – at least while the attention's on him.

The effect's only slightly undermined later when he admits that he once went for the captaincy of Middlesex 'because it was worth a few extra quid', but the management quietly pulled him aside and said, 'We don't really think that's you, Tuffers.'

If anyone's going to steal the limelight from Phil on his birthday, though, it's Catalina. The public have voted for her to face today's Trial and she looks like Mrs Ceausescu must have when she realized the approaching firing squad meant the Romanian people were less keen on her and her hubby than she'd thought.

'Bastards!' Cat's heard to hiss, rather unwisely, given that she's talking about the people who hold her immediate future in the palm of their hands – but she shouldn't take it to heart.

Even if 100 per cent of the British population voted for her, probably only half meant her any real harm, and the other half just wanted to see her stuffing frogs down her bikini, or whatever else the pervy producers had in store.

Still, it must have helped her to know that her fellow celebs were right behind her. 'The walk of death!' Antony shouts helpfully as she begins the slow walk across the bridge to the Trial Area and to her designated torture – the 'Croc Pit'.

As the name suggests, this is simply a pit – well actually it's a lake; what are they talking about? – that may, or may not, be full to the brim with malevolent crocodiles.

Much later in the day, after a few drinks, one of the

off-duty production team (clearly working in a more authentic area like insect husbandry) was heard to scoff, 'That was rubbish. Most of the crocodiles were obviously animatronic.'

Cat may not have known that but she probably had faith in the first lesson that everyone learns at TV school: do not let the talent be devoured by giant reptiles.

The producers might have got away with Antony's near decapitation by the falling plant – no one liked him much anyway – but Cat's grisly death by crocodile would have looked a little too preventable. Surely there must be more safeguards on offer than just the stern looking security guard holding the tranquillizer gun.

Even so, watching her stride into the water, it's not hard to suspend disbelief a little. Catalina's permanent pout means that relatively few facial expressions are available to her (mostly those involving sex, sulking and her own unique combination of both) but she makes a good stab at Fash's terrified-but-noble look.

Before the series started she'd said she wanted to be like Lara Croft, but in her bikinied shimmy through the pool she's more like a low-rent Ursula Andress, slinking out of the sea in *Dr No*. In fact, it was probably the crocs who were more scared. After all, this is the celeb who famously said that she flirted with anything: 'men, women … even animals'.

Today may not have been the first time she'd cosied up to reptiles in search of a free lunch, but the results were nevertheless impressive: she picked up all ten stars from the water; the celebs would celebrate Phil's birthday with ten fresh meals; and maybe there'd be something extra for him, too. Wouldn't there? Um …

Phil had been having another good day so far. His attempt to explain the laws of cricket to Linda is not much short of heroic, becoming increasingly elementary-school when he realizes that to talk about 'runs' or 'wickets' would probably be to get a little too technical. 'You hit a six, and everyone goes "Woooh!",' he finishes cheerfully.

'Are you a fast bowler?' Linda asks.

'No, I'm a slow bowler.'

'Ha!' she laughs, obviously assuming that lazy old Tuffers just can't be bothered to bowl quickly.

And then a message arrives by Bush Telegraph. The celebs are offered three bottles of wine, as a treat in honour of Phil's birthday, in exchange for three of the meals that Cat won.

'The hardest decision … of his life,' Ant and Dec announce melodramatically, but is it? Of course they'll take the wine, won't they? So far boredom seems to have been more of a problem than malnutrition, and Phil's never been in Australia for this long without drinking before. Even during a long innings bowling at Steve Waugh, he probably had a hip flask.

To begin with, it looks like a fairly straightforward decision, but then some faint, slightly sullen voices of dissent emerge. Danniella and Fash don't drink and most of the others are none too keen, either.

'It's not the end of the world. I'd rather everyone else had some food,' Phil shrugs.

The other celebs look uncomfortable. Most of them

THE VIEW FROM THE BOTTOM! Deep in the bowels of their volcanic crater, the celebs couldn't see these bridges.

Eight of our hapless celebs gathered in London clutching blow-up spiders and toy snakes… it was just a matter of time before they confronted the real thing! At this stage, Catalina and Toyah were still umming and ahhing, and who can blame them?

Catalina (left) and Toyah (above) look pretty happy as they arrive in Australia, little imagining the devilish tortures awaiting them.

While our ten unsuspecting stars live it up on the Gold Coast, Ant and Dec explore the camp and meet a few of the inhabitants.

The gang settle in and get all touchy feely with a group massage. Ahhhh.

Danniella and Toyah discover how hard life in the jungle can be. But while Toyah finds her trials exciting, Danniella is finding a life without her family and chocolate very hard to bear.

Heroes and villains. Fash, the all-round jungle hero, strides to meet his worst fears. While down below, Chris has his sights firmly set on Cat.

Just another night in the jungle. The terrible trio beg for more booze and fags.

Celebration time as the troops entertain themselves with an all-singing all-dancing display.

DANGER!!!
Antony narrowly misses being knocked out by
a malicious falling branch. While Toyah searches
for creepy crawlies in Phil's hair.

clearly want to say, 'Bollocks to the wine, I'm hungry!' But instead they mutter resentfully about its being his decision. As soon as he's wandered off in the direction of the Bush Telegraph hut, though, their real feelings come out. 'Ten meals Catalina got us,' Fash complains quietly, 'and we're about to waste it on alcohol.' The rest of them sit there stewing silently, thinking dark thoughts.

Meanwhile, at the hut, Phil is going through a moral crisis. 'Oh, shit, man,' he moans, clutching his head, 'I could do with a glass of wine. What colour's the wine?'

It doesn't make any difference. Whether it's because he's more calculating than he looks and he's thinking about how it'll play at home, or because he just wants to do the right thing, Phil gives in and turns the wine down. Greater love hath no man … and all that.

But there are other arguments brewing. After two days of just one meal a day, Wayne is as mad as hell and he's not going to take it any more. Well, actually, he just looks a little miffed, and there's not much he can do about it; but, for the first time, tension is clearly rising.

'I don't mind sitting around all day waiting for a meal,' Wayne says, rather bizarrely, as the whole reason they're having the conversation is that he *does* mind.

'I can't believe we're having an argument about rice and beans,' replies Antony evenly.

Luckily, though, Phil is once again on hand to diffuse the situation – this time with the magic weapon of saying something really stupid and pointless. 'I don't think we should eat at all,' he says, mugging wildly.

'That's helpful,' Wayne mutters, through gritted

teeth, but for the time being the storm clouds have passed.

They return only when Danniella Westbrook hits her own emotional wall. And, unfortunately, her wall seems a lot closer than everybody else's. In fact it's debatable whether she's ever managed to reverse out of her emotional garage.

Cruel? Of course it's cruel. In some ways Danni's been the most interesting character of them all so far: a weird, confused child-mother.

Her unique mixture of the matter-of-fact and the deeply strange was emphasized in one of the most blankly surreal moments yesterday when she announced that she didn't like rice. 'I've only had it once,' she said nonchalantly. 'And I didn't like it.'

Huh? How can you not like rice?

But, anyway, her appearance in the Bush Telegraph hut was the most emotional moment of the programme so far. Even if you wanted to slap her to start with you couldn't help but sympathize when she sobbed, 'I miss Kevin, and the children – and [an even bigger sob] I miss chocolate!'

Not necessarily in that order, presumably.

Of course there's a danger that Danniella's crisis could encourage the other celebs to have their own little breakdown.

Toyah has already made a preliminary bid, staring into space and saying, 'I'm just having a miss-my-husband moment.'

Those are the kinds of moments that absolutely have

to be catching because otherwise the other celebs' spouses sitting back at the hotel will be thinking, Hey, why isn't he/she missing me that much? When do I get my emotional breakdown?

Expect more turmoil to come ...

Quote of the day

Danniella in the Bush Telegraph hut: 'I miss Kevin, and the children – and [a big sob] I miss chocolate.'

Day Three

If Day Two was when the celebs started seething silently, Day Three is when the seething became an audible, ear-bending hum. The producers had turned the cruelty amps up to eleven and the celebs were slowly, or in some cases quickly, falling apart.

Already one of the central truths of reality TV is starting to emerge: what looks good in the confines of the set may not look quite so good to the people watching at home. For example: the other celebs seem to be immune to the sheer ludicrousness of Fash's endless motivational speeches, his ability to make being scared of absolutely everything look like heroism, and his exaggerated military metaphors. ('We're in Vietnam, man. You can't start questioning the food,' he says at one point, with scant regard for geography or indeed cookery.)

They still seem to regard him as a kind of leader by default, though, even if he's not officially in charge. So far every day has started with his taking an exercise class and they all obediently join in: rolling their heads backwards and forwards and stretching their limbs like a bunch of browbeaten members of Weight Watchers.

At one point, when he's giving Catalina a friendly neck massage, she does look as if she's thinking, Move those hands any lower down and I'll do to you what I did to those crocs, buster! But on the whole they seem to be remarkably tolerant of him.

When Phil and Sian manage to get lost in the middle of the night (on the way back from the toilet, they claim), it's Fash they call for to help them find their way back home. He's never entirely lost the heroic glow he gained on the first day – but judging by the press back home he's less of a hero to the public.

Antony WT, on the other hand, comes across on TV as being quite a reasonable chap. Can you really hate someone who's got so many stories that end with variations on 'and I never got a chance to say goodbye' 'so that's when I tried to throw myself in front of the jumbo jet' 'they punched me in the face first, and then the ribs' 'and that's when the dog fell into the printing press'? (Well, at least three of these are genuine.)

Even Danniella's attempt to trump him with the story of her drug hell and brief marriage – 'Who's that guy staring at me?' she apparently once asked, only to be told, 'That's your ex-husband!' – doesn't quite have the same mixture of implausible bad luck and horrible violence. Don't the other celebs realize they need their daily wallow in someone else's misery?

If you just watched the main evening programme you

might get the impression that their days are highly eventful. Oh, no. Most of their day is spent telling each other their life stories and Antony has probably got the most interesting life story of all.

They all sit there listening, rapt – but when they sneak off in pairs it's very different. Are they grateful that he's doing all the cooking? That he's the only celeb who's indisputably improving the quality of their lives in some small way, even if it's only by knowing the correct length of time to boil rice? Um, no.

'We're not on *Ready Steady Cook*, honey!' Wayne bitches to Danniella.

The Bush Dog was right. Somehow Antony WT just manages to get under people's skin. Happily, though, he seems completely oblivious. 'They're all obsessing about food,' he beams, rather missing what they're *really* obsessing about, 'but I don't really need it. I'm quite chuffed that there isn't any food 'cos I need to lose this.' He pats his large stomach and waddles cheerfully off to prepare yet another meal for the ungrateful celebs to wolf down: a task that's become even harder with their first failure in a Bush Tucker Trial.

'Dancers aren't that popular, I knew that,' Wayne murmured poignantly when he heard the news that the public had voted for him to face the horrendous 'Rat Food Suit' trial. But he's missing the point, just as Catalina missed the point. The public haven't chosen him because they dislike him, any more than a curious child dislikes a daddy longlegs as they're tearing its legs off. The public don't have a grudge against you, Wayne.

They just think it'll be funny to watch you suffer. It's kind of a compliment if you think about it.

Still, there must have been some twinges of conscience in living rooms across the land when they saw what the tiny dancer had to go through. With horrible irony he dealt with having rats swarm all over him, only to be denied by the fact that he could find only two of the keys, buried cruelly deep in the gravel.

Of course the ten of them had agreed right at the start that they wouldn't bitch if anyone failed a trial. They'd remember that, wouldn't they?

'We're all good lads; no one's going to blame him,' says Antony afterwards, remarkably squeezing three factual errors into ten words.

Cut to a grim-faced Fash unashamedly prepared to look like the most callous man in the universe. 'If you're not scared of rats, which you're obviously not, why did you only get two keys?' he asks with barely concealed bitterness.

In a day of serious bad luck they even manage to lose out on some valuable seasoning for their food by getting the celebrity-chest question wrong – 'Which Minogue sister has highlighted her pert posterior with a tattoo?' – despite setting up an Old Bailey-style court to debate it.

As you'd expect, Fash is the judge, although with a pair of boxer shorts wrapped around his head he looks more like someone angling for a demob on the grounds of mental instability.

Only Linda and Antony really make the case for the

younger Minogue sister. Linda, in particular, emphasizes her essential sensibleness by putting forward some pretty strong arguments. 'If it was Kylie, we'd know!' she points out irrefutably.

'Danni's always had a smaller arse, if you want to look at it,' says Antony with a scientific air. 'I went with her in a car from Liverpool, once,' he explains, raising visions of the portly chef 'accidentally' dropping his Murray Mints by the car door and asking Danni to pick them up for him.

But the Kylie lobby are too strong and they lose out once again. 'We really tried to make the first questions easy!' the Granada question writer says in near despair afterwards.

Still, the other Danni seems to be putting a braver face on things. 'We've got face paints,' Danniella sighs stoically, when they find out what the second prize is.

Maybe it helps that she's at last projecting some of her anger outwards rather than inwards. She, Wayne and Sian have given up being discreet! 'I find with some people it's "lights, camera, action!"' Wayne moans. 'It's driving me crazy.'

'I've reached the stage where I don't care,' adds Sian. 'For f***'s sake be yourselves.'

But it seems Catalina has committed the ultimate unforgivable sin. At the start, the celebs were all given a supply of salt to burn away the leeches but, unfortunately, because they got the Danni/Kylie question wrong, they haven't managed to acquire any more.

'I watched her putting salt all over her own food,'

Danniella snipes. 'But it's better not to say anything, just let her get on with it. I want to say, "Oi, sort yourself out!"'

Maybe Toyah's made the right decision by drifting off into her own world of Zen-like serenity. Before the series started she was the one who spouted all the usual clichés about 'finding' herself with the most sincerity and, weirdly, it seems that she was actually telling the truth.

She hardly seems to notice that there's a TV programme going on, so absorbed is she in becoming a kind of freakishly calm and intensely practical Amazonian jungle queen. To his immense pride, she even makes Fash her 'second-in-command' when Tuffers declares her leader.

Where Fash was an inspirational sergeant major of a leader, and Phil saw his job as keeping the peace and making everyone laugh, Toyah seems to see her role as a more practical one: Getting. Things. Done.

Even so, the intrusion of reality in her little bubble of positive thinking is a frightening experience. One of her first jobs is to announce to the other celebs that they have to empty the toilets. Relatively straightforward, you'd have thought. To Toyah, though, it's an extraordinary suggestion and she can barely read the instructions because she's laughing so hard.

Luckily, at this stage the celebs are still trying to be good sports and she's inundated with volunteers. 'I should do it,' says Wayne dejectedly. ''Cos I only got two meals.'

But the other celebs are already getting slightly bored

with his self-imposed martyrdom and they practically trample him underfoot in a rush for the dunny.

Will they be quite so keen in the days ahead?

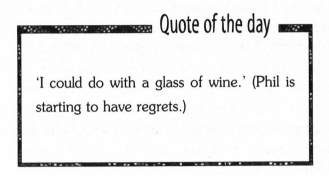

Quote of the day

'I could do with a glass of wine.' (Phil is starting to have regrets.)

The digital-free viewer's guide to what didn't make the main programme

Just what exactly have they been doing for the first three days?

Sleeping: 30 per cent of the time.

Cooking: 0 per cent of the time (except Antony, obviously).

Eating: 1 per cent of the time.

Talking about eating: 10 per cent of the time.

Talking about bowel movements: 20 per cent of the time.

Having bowel movements: 0.001 per cent of the time (estimate).

Telling good jokes: 0.001 per cent of the time.

Telling bad jokes: 1 per cent of the time.

Flirting: 3 per cent of the time.

Doing chores: 7 per cent of the time.

Bitching to each other's face: 0.001 per cent of the time.

Bitching behind each other's back: 1 per cent of the time.

Staring aimlessly into space: 20 per cent of the time.

Arguing about what day it is: 1 per cent of the time. (You'd be surprised how long it took them to work out whether they should be on UK time or Australia time. They sang 'Happy Birthday' to Phil for two days running.)

PLUS ...

Chris: Play-fighting with Catalina in a boyish attempt at flirtation. Dropping things (Chris is somewhat gauche).

Antony: Cooking. Telling his life story.

Catalina: Cruelly indulging Chris's flirtations. Painting with the face paints they 'won'.

Wayne: Bitching with and/or comforting Danniella. Dancing. Telling showbiz anecdotes.

Danniella: Bitching to Wayne. Crying. Missing family. Sucking thumb.

Toyah: Growing as a person. Becoming spiritually one with nature. Etc. etc. etc.

Sian: Sympathising intensely with everyone like some kind of Welsh Sybil Fawlty ('Ooh, I know!').

Phil: Laconically indulging Linda and Sian's flirting. Telling even more jokes, like this one: 'A bear goes into a bar and says, "I'd like a pint of beer and [long pause] a packet of crisps, please." And the barman says, "Why the long pause?" [Raises bear hands.] "I'm a bear, aren't I?"'

Linda: Doing craft stuff, including baskets, a mosaic next to Chris's bed, tiles for the dunny floor, a clothes rack (there's a woman who really loves her day job).

John: Practising his martial arts. Talking about martial arts.

Day Four

Today starts, as so many days do, with Super Fash taking one for the team, stepping up to the plate and generally being his all-round heroic self. However, even his titanium-plated positivity has been dented by the news that the public have voted for him to take a second trial – at the Bridge of Doom.

'You like to think it's 'cos people want to see you again,' he murmurs, without much conviction.

As we've intimated before, though, the main reason is that the British public are basically evil. If you tell them that you're scared of heights, then of course they're going to nominate you to take a trial that involves hanging upside down off a rope bridge like some kind of rainforest Harold Lloyd.

And give Fash his dues: he gives good drama. You get the feeling that, if his trial were to down a glass of water, he'd do a few kung fu kicks and stare intensely into space first.

Which brings us to the first big talking point of the

series so far: is Fash really scared of heights, or does he just put it on so it looks more impressive when he 'conquers' his fear?

Tara Palmer-Tompkinson is convinced it's the latter. 'You can't pull the cashmere over my eyes. I think he's a bit afraid of heights, like anyone would be. But really afraid? No!'

Chris Lore, the trials supervisor who designed the Bridge of Doom, agrees. 'We actually made it easier for him and I think he bamboozled us. The first day it took him ages just to walk over the bridge to the Trial Area and he was talking to himself all the way, but when he got to the Bridge of Doom he practically ran across!'

To be fair to poor old Fash, though, maybe he really *is* scared of heights (and insects, snakes, bunny rabbits, fluffy clouds and so on) and maybe he really has conquered his fear. You shouldn't underestimate the will to win of a man who once tackled someone (Gary Mabbutt) so hard that the Tottenham captain's teammates genuinely thought he was dead.

Either way, Fash's fellow celebs wouldn't have cared if he'd grown up in the circus, swinging across the big top and catching acrobats in his teeth. He brought them back another eight meals. Hurrah! Go, Fash! And so on!

You could tell the difference, too. The celebs (like most of us) like to believe that their emotions are deep, spiritual things but that theory is undermined by a couple of celebrity equations:

- Big meal = nice, happy, smiley celebs
- Small meal = mean, sad, pouty celebs

Today was the day when the volcanic eruptions of Day Three settled back to a warm, mellow rumble. Before that could happen, though, there had to be one last puff of smoke.

It started when Chris realized that he needed to up his profile somewhat. So far his typical day had included laughing at everyone else's jokes and looking slightly out of place, but not much else. Luckily an opportunity to make a bit of a splash was just around the corner. On a rock, down by the pool, a temptingly unclothed Catalina was busy drying her long, shiny hair.

In the last couple of days she'd begun removing a layer of clothes every day and she was wearing a brief, sarong-style miniskirt and a black bikini − irresistible to a man who'd spent the last four years in *Coronation Street* (where Ena Sharples was always considered a bit of a babe).

In retrospect, his mistake was to think that it was Catalina who needed to cool off. Big-game-hunter style, he got her in his sights with his water pistol and let rip with a stream of cold water. Unfortunately, his attack didn't have quite the desired effect (something along the lines of, 'Oh Chris you're so playful and yet masculine with your big gun. Shall we have sex now?')

'I don't mind having water fights and everything,' she lied, shaking her wet hair irritably. 'But I just got dry.'

You can see her point. In the social whirl of camp life there's very little time for trivial things like drying your hair, what with the 25°C temperature most of the time and having hours and hours just to lie around in the sun.

'I'm not in the doghouse, am I?' Chris asks dolefully.

'No, of course you're not,' she snaps. (Celeb-speak can be a little confusing until you're used to it. For some reason they often say exactly the opposite to what they mean. Or is that just feminine grammar?)

Anyway, the little episode did them both good.

Chris realized that Catalina wasn't the type of girl who'd appreciate a playful, tentative kind of flirtation and in the process he looked a bit less of a wimp. 'I'm just going to see if Cat's put her dummy back in,' he grins to Antony and Danniella.

Cat, for her part, realized that she'd gone a little too far with the superbitch, um, act. For the rest of the day she spent her time assiduously building bridges with the other female celebs. In a particularly poignant moment, her old friend Danniella says, 'I'm just not used to you being this loud,' suggesting that Catalina's not normally like this. She might even be a nice person in real life.

'I didn't know if I was annoying everybody, or not,' Cat says plaintively.

Danniella tugs at her hair and swallows hard. 'You're not. Don't get paranoid.'

They hug.

After that it's Sian's turn and, happily, she manages to spend several hours talking about relationships with Cat without ever looking as if she finds the model annoying. But then Sian would probably find some way to sympathize with Pol Pot ('I know! Those f***ing skulls! They just get everywhere, don't they!')

Finally, if the water attack slowed down Catalina's day-by-day striptease, it had to be a good thing. She'd have been down to her lower intestines by the time the week was out.

Even more happy vibes were in the air for the camp chef (in every sense), Antony. First, Linda gave him a vote of confidence at the celebrity chest. 'I was really glad when he was asked to be Chest Partner with me,' she beamed. 'He's great fun.'

And, at last, someone put a word in for his cooking skills. 'We'd have been snookered without Antony here,' Chris says matter-of-factly.

There's a brief, slightly grudging moment while the others consider this point and then they're forced to agree. 'I couldn't believe what he did with that rice,' Wayne admits. 'It's not what chefs can do with gourmet food. It's what they can do with nothing.'

THE wonderful world OF Worrall

Antony Worrall Thompson has got millions of stories. Some of them may even be true. This is just one of them ...

THE DAY ANTONY ATTACKED A POLICEMAN ...

WAYNE: Have you ever been arrested?

ANTONY: Yes, I have. The Australians [immigration] always give me a hard time, even though it was twenty years ago.

WAYNE: What? Even when you came in this time?

ANTONY: Yes. (Matter-of-factly) I beat up a policeman once.

Linda squeals.

SIAN: How old were you?

ANTONY: I was twenty-nine. You remember I told you about my *ménage a troi*? And the girl? Well we'd just celebrated moving in together.

SIAN: Hubby was off the scene?

ANTONY: Yes, hubby was off the scene. We'd got pissed, OK, and we'd decided to go to the Embassy Club.

WAYNE (delighted and shocked): You used to go to the Embassy Club?

ANTONY: In my little shorts! I had a pink leather catsuit at one stage. A pink leather catsuit that zipped from there (points to feet) to there (points to neck).

CHRIS: No wonder you're the camp chef!

ANTONY: Well, it was a gay club. You'd get funny looks if you didn't dress like everyone else.

EVERYONE: 'No'; 'You're winding us up' (etc.),

ANTONY: It was a laugh. It was the place to go on a Sunday night. Anyway, we went round there and we were sort of playing tag on the way. And I said to the girl, 'We better behave ourselves, there's two policemen coming.' But we were giggling and I'm so stupid. I said, 'Officer, please tell this woman to stop following me.' And he suddenly went all nasty: 'You've been abusing this woman. I'm arresting you for breach of the peace.' And he grabbed me. I said, 'Hey, you don't have to touch me. Just talk to me. OK – sense-of-humour failure. I'm sorry, I apologize.'

WAYNE: It wasn't because of what you were wearing, was it?

ANTONY: No, I wasn't in the pink leather then. He grabbed me again and I just lost it. I picked him up and we went bundling over and I heard his fingers crack. And I still remember this line, it was so funny: he was shouting to this rookie who was with him, 'Call for assistance! Call for assistance!' And the rookie said, 'I don't know how to work the radio!'

Everyone displays hilarity.

But then of course it was Antony's birthday today, so he deserved a little respect. Not that any would be forthcoming from outside the camp. Just like Phil, he was forced to make a cruel choice – either he could take a handmade birthday card from his family, or a bottle of wine, a bottle of coke and some spices.

With a brief gulp and a couple of quickly wiped-away tears, he opts to do the right thing for the team. Unsurprisingly, the other celebs agree with his decision. 'He's made the right choice,' says Danniella senti-mentally. 'If I saw a card from my family now I'd cry and want to go home.'

Fash, however, is a little more practical. 'What kind of choice was that?' he demands. 'Ten people in the jungle all hungry, or a card! What?!'

Still, the only real outbreak of nastiness today comes from one of the producers' little jokes. Late at night the celebs discover something on one of the tree stumps. 'Is that mould,' Linda asks, 'or is it loads of spider webs?'

In fact, it's mould. Before they let the celebs into the camp the cruel producers threw yoghurt over that stump in a kind of twisted experiment to see how quickly something would grow there. In the heat of the jungle it didn't take long at all. With the camp getting on relatively well today, though, will they need to resort to similarly dirty tricks in the days to come?

Quote of the day

'It's like if you're asked, "How big's your willy?" men always say ten inches when they know perfectly well it's only four.' Antony gives a bit too much away during the celebrity-chest debate.

Chris's guide to the trials: Part I

TRIAL ONE: KEEP IT IN YOUR PANTS

Contestant: Fash

'I've modelled those pants many times, I wouldn't ask them to do something I wouldn't do myself, and, even though I'm quite used to it, that's still an uncomfortable trial.

'The cockroaches are the worst. They can climb anything and they're so fast – it's pretty horrible when one skitters over your neck.

'The yabbies [crayfish] were probably pinching Fash, too. Their pincers are really sharp but they're the right size – they're too small to break the skin.'

TRIAL TWO: THE CROC PIT

Contestant: Catalina

'I think she knew the big croc wasn't real. She had to

91

know. For anyone to jump into the water with a crocodile that size they'd have to be crazy. She'd probably seen the tapes of the US show.

'Nikki Schieler Ziering [American model], who did the Croc Pit in the US *Celebrity*, barely even got into the water. She came back in tears saying, "It's full of crocodiles and there's a man with a gun!"

'The other celebs had this big meeting about it, they were saying [tough-guy American actor voice], "This time I think the producers have gone a step too far." There were seven real crocs in there but they were only babies. They could give someone a knock with their tail but they wouldn't bite you.

'This is the biggest smoke-and-mirrors trial but Catalina didn't fall for it. She was either very brave or she had inside information.'

TRIAL THREE: RAT FOOD SUIT

Contestant: Wayne

'Everyone who's been down to the Trial Area has been fun, and Wayne was great. The rats were all over him, knocking his glasses off, and he didn't say anything, he didn't complain at all.

'I felt bad for him when he only got two stars. We told him to dig away the debris but I think he was being a bit too tentative.'

TRIAL FOUR: BRIDGE OF DOOM

Contestant: Fash

'I try to design all the trials so that they can be done by a man or a woman, someone of any physical ability. When we know who's going to take part we can adjust the time limit or whatever.

'I did the Bridge of Doom in about two minutes twenty seconds, but then I knew what was going to happen. We had a few people do it and then we based how long we'd give them on an average of that.

'If it's a strong guy we thought it would probably be a three-minute game. If they were not quite so strong we'd have given them four minutes. When we found out it was Fash, knowing how long it'd taken him to get over the normal bridge, we gave him five minutes.

'Now, having seen it, and knowing a bit more what he's like, I think he conned us! He ran across that thing. He did it in about four minutes twenty-seven.'

Day Five

Something odd happened within the camp today. During the night, in a Big-style series of role reversals, the personalities of some of our celebs seem to have migrated between their different hammocks.

Fash, who'd been so positive and energetic, is suddenly gloomy and sombre. The effect of being nominated for the Bush Tucker Trial again yesterday seems to have hit him hard. Even his martial-arts training doesn't give him so much pleasure any more. Every day he'd been getting a step closer to one of the trees and today it really looked as if he was going to cause it some serious damage.

'Fash is now fighting with trees,' Sian whispers, with just a trace of mockery that would have been unthinkable a day or two before.

'There's no sugar, which people need in their daily diet,' he rationalizes. 'You'll see a change of mood and character from all of us. We can put a smile on our face but you'll see changes.'

Linda certainly seems to have changed. Or at least that's what the others think. When she takes over the leadership baton from Chris, she sees it as an opportunity to improve all their lives with a few commonsense innovations. Unfortunately, the rest of them aren't so keen on her ideas – or at least on the way she proposes them.

They'll accept being bossed around by the Fash, because, well, he's the Fash. But when Linda starts throwing her weight around that's another thing entirely. The big man decides to have words with her. 'You know what they say about a good referee?' he points out haughtily. 'A good referee is a referee you don't see!'

If Fash were a referee he'd have a flashing police light on his head and distress flares flying out of his ears, but, not for the first time, he's saying what everyone else is thinking.

'You mean you don't want to see me?' Linda asks, deflated.

Even her new friend Antony starts calling her 'Miss Whiplash' and tries to point out gently that she's putting a few backs up. 'They were a bit shocked with you to begin with,' he says.

'Seriously?'

'Well, not seriously, seriously but …'

She gets the point.

Even more bizarrely, Phil seems to have been taking a few lessons from Wayne and Antony. At times, wobbling backwards and forwards as he speaks and rubbing his hands over his lop-sided face, he resembles

Zippy, the somewhat camp puppet from the children's TV show *Rainbow*.

'You were the one who was calling Wayne "darling" last night,' Sian says to Phil.

'I know,' he sighs. 'And Antony called me "babe". The camp chef is catching.'

The biggest change, though, has been experienced by Danniella. Her clear-the-air chat with Catalina has given her a spring to her step and indeed to her cleavage, which she's now wielding with a new *joi de vivre*. 'I'll put everyone's stuff under your beds, otherwise it'll get soaked,' she says cheerfully as the rain starts to fall first thing in the morning. 'I'll put yours there, Cat.'

'Thanks, love,' says Catalina, bemused but grateful.

Even the fact that Danniella has to take the day's Bush Tucker trial – 'Catch a Falling Star' – doesn't dampen her spirits. If anything, the prospect of being drenched in various kinds of insect hell seems to make her even more cheerful. For the first time Ant and Dec are put on the back foot as she flirts with them, trials supervisor Chris Lore and Dr Bob with a sassy swagger that makes Cat look amateurish.

Unfortunately, Dr Bob isn't in her good books for long. The celebs have always seemed to trust the kindly-looking medic. He's there at all the trials, giving them sage advice and making sure they don't come to any harm; but, for the first time, they realize that he may not entirely be on their side.

'I shouldn't tell you this while the camera's on,' he

whispers conspiratorially, 'but you should try to get the eel slime all over your face – the other critters don't like it.'

Poor, sweet, innocent Danniella nods eagerly. The first box opens and several pints of eel jelly pour over her head and she rubs it around her face to make sure it's quite covered. Surely with the magic slime on her face the nasty creepy-crawlies in the other boxes will take one sniff and then creep disgustedly away, won't they?

Um, no. Instead the slime acts as a kind of glue and everything else that comes down sticks to her skin, especially the feathers. 'They're going to cook her when she gets back,' Ant jokes. 'They'll think she's a bush turkey. Antony will be getting her on the fire.'

When she gets back to the camp, sadly with just three stars, Danniella proves that she's smarter than she looks. 'Dr Bob's not looking after our interests!' she announces, outraged. 'He said, "Get as much of that eel stuff over your face as you can, 'cos the other insects don't like it". So of course me being a dumb blonde, I put it all over meself and all the other insects stuck to me. He's a proper wrong 'un. I was running all over with beasts!'

'I told her half the truth,' says Bob, somewhat disingenuously. 'What I said to Danniella, which was true, was that if she got the slime all over her face the insects wouldn't be able to scratch her. The cockroaches could give you a nasty scratch but the slime prevented that. I just didn't tell her that it would make everything else that came down stick to her!'

What was in the boxes?

Box One: Eel slime. Carefully extracted by hand (well, that's what the eel handlers say, but I bet the eels don't think they're being all that careful).

Box Two: Meal worms. A larval form of beetle, these little critters, who presumably didn't choose their own name, are apparently tasty when boiled.

Box Three: Bush cockroaches. Like regular roaches, only bigger.

Box Four: Crickets. Noisy little insects who spend the day trying to shelter from the elements in any warm crevice. Much like English cricketers.

Box Five: Turkey feathers. For that tarred-and-feathered effect.

It seems likely that what most riles Danniella, though, is when Bob approaches her with a towel to wipe her clean. She raises her arms happily over her head so that he can remove as many of the bugs as possible and he dabs carefully at a tiny area around her goggles.

Danniella is left to wander back to camp with the feathers covering her – but, then, she does look, um, strangely attractive like that. Phil certainly seems to think so. Predictably house-proud, Linda sternly forbids Danniella from jumping in the pool to wash off (a few more weeks there and she'd have had them taking their shoes off before they entered the camp) but chivalrous Tuffers wastes no time, jumping in fully clothed with her, and affectionately dousing her with water.

For all the minor backbiting of the day, though, the celebs have once again managed to defy predictions that they'd constantly be at each other's throat. *Down* each other's throat might be more accurate in Danniella and Catalina's case, as the two friends make up by swapping fruit in a tabloid-teasing snog. Chris watches stoically.

Camp might even be doing some of them good. 'I'm missing a drink a bit, actually,' Phil says, only half joking. 'I'm starting to think I might be an alcoholic.'

The day finishes with a serious discussion about substance abuse between Fash and Sian. 'I don't know any drug addicts at all,' Sian says, to the immense relief of the Met Office back in London. 'No one ever offers me drugs. I must give off an aura that I'm not interested.'

Fash nods eagerly. 'No one even offers me alcohol!'

I guess he gives off an aura too. Unfortunately it seems that the public have picked up on it.

Quote of the day

'They're all in me bristols, look!' Ant and Dec happily take up Danniella's invitation to look at her 'beasts'.

Day Six

Day Six was the moment when Sian and Phil started to look a little uncomfortable and edgy. You might think this was because Day Six was also the day when the fragile rules of the camp were rudely shattered and Antony revealed his crazy, anarchic side.

But no: apparently it was because they hadn't yet 'changed their shoes'. For a while, the producers couldn't work out what the celebs meant by that. It was clearly some kind of code, but code for what?

Given that later on in the evening Phil and Antony staged the show's first mutiny, they could have been forgiven for wondering whether it was all part of a daring escape plan. Maybe 'changing their shoes' meant 'breaking camp, stealing the chopper and heading back to the Versace'.

But that can't be right, because only Sian and Phil haven't done it yet. And the others are taking bets on when they're going to do it. It's not a sexual thing is, it? Chris and Linda have changed their shoes. Fash and Antony have changed their shoes. Ughhh!

The first clue comes when Antony confidently puts a tenner on Phil to be the last one to do the deed. As the chef, he's got a little inside knowledge in certain areas. In fact, you wonder whether he could have doctored Phil's food in order to make that bet a dead cert.

Because, while on an American show 'changing your shoes' would have referred to some emergency silicon-implant maintenance, and on a French show it would've referred to a group orgy, this is Britain, so inevitably they're talking about bowel movements. (On an Australian show they'd just have said 'taking a shit'.)

And if Day Six was the point when the celebs' obsession with their own bodily functions reached crisis point, it was noticeable that Fash was never one of those worrying. With the public cruelly probing every one of his 'phobias', it was more likely that he'd have the opposite problem. Especially when he was nominated, for a gut-wrenching third time, to take on a Bush Tucker. And this time it was the Snake Pit.

If he'd been crying wolf before, his fear at this trial looks more believable.

'If a snake goes into an S-Bend, it's preparing to strike,' Bob tells him. 'If it's lying flat, you don't have anything to worry about.'

Fash looks, once again, as if he needs to visit an S-bend or a U-bend himself.

'Their teeth point backwards,' Bob continues. 'If one of them bites you they won't let go. The best thing you can do is grab its tail and just wait for us to come and get it off.'

Understandably, even Super Fash struggles with this trial. Moving very, very slowly, he manages to gather just four stars as time runs out. And, as the snakes are starting to take a closer interest in what he's up to, Fash is probably relieved to be able to leave.

But, if the public don't like him, the snakes seem very keen indeed. 'He's pretty close to you, that one,' Dec says, with masterful understatement as one of them wraps itself round Fash's right leg like a reptilian Vinnie Jones.

The lack of food they receive today once again takes its toll towards the evening. Antony seems the happiest of them, maybe because he's the only one of the celebs to have fat reserves to burn up. 'I found a rib today,' he says feeling under his arm. 'I haven't felt that rib for years.'

The change in Antony is indeed miraculous. When he arrived, puffing on a fag in an unflattering blue vest, he looked like the bastard offspring of Big Daddy and Waynetta Slob, but he seems to have shed a chin a day. Lucky he had plenty of chins to lose. Fash's exercise regime, meanwhile, has reached crazily obsessive levels. Today he breaks his record of 353 sit-ups, but he's looking painfully gaunt and strained.

'At the moment, exercise is what we live for,' Fash says. The others look at him askance. Um, 'we', Fash?

But kindly Linda takes pity on him. 'I do love those exercises in the morning,' she volunteers.

If on previous days the celebs have turned on each other, today is when they turn on the producers and even the whole concept of being a 'celebrity'. In a series of fireside confessions they're asked to talk about what they've learned from the experience of life in the camp. Instead of the obvious things (the effects of a diet of rice and beans on the digestive system, the immense importance of deodorant), they get Deep. And Moving.

Even the snakes slithering through the jungle nearby are blinking back tears as Antony talks about how his shyness is mistaken for arrogance and Danniella says that she just wants to be with her family. Ahhh …

Most extraordinarily, Catalina says she doesn't want to be a celebrity any more. ('Yeah!' say the snakes, shedding their skins, 'I don't want to be a snake any more, either … Oh, damn! There's another snake underneath!')

'The whole celebrity thing is a load of bullshit,' Cat says. 'People really manipulate you and I'm really fed up with it and I refuse to do it any more. When I get out I'm only going do what I want to do and try to keep away from anything tabloidy.

'I've had to do it all because I've needed the money,' she continues. 'I want to get back in control … I prefer the quiet life and I'm not into the celebrity lifestyle. I want to settle down and have a family really, really soon – so can Mr Right come along really soon, please?' she begs. 'I want to have children and I want to make things and be really, really silly with them. I want a house and a farm and a big studio where I can paint things.'

Ahhh – again. To give Catalina her dues, by this point she has had to spend a week with people constantly going on about how great kids and marriage are. As a form of rehab, she should go and stay for a week or so with Danniella and Kevin, or Antony and Jacinta, and see what it's really like.

It should be pointed out that the celebs have been given two bottles of wine this evening, but, judging by the state Antony, Linda and (especially) Phil manages to get into, the rest of them didn't even get a sniff.

It all started, as these things so often do, with our three heroes becoming increasingly garrulous. In the Bush Telegraph hut they at last open up and let their fellow celebs know exactly what they think of them. Last year, they'd have been mopping bile off the hut floor for weeks afterwards, but this time things are a little different. Antony causes a few intakes of breath by spotting the link between 'Fash' and 'Fascist' (do you see what he's done there?).

But he qualifies the statement by pointing out, 'He's a great leader isn't he? He is great. He is perfect for his role in life as a diplomat.'

And Phil weighs in, as though preparing to deliver a few kicks to Wayne's diminutive frame. 'I don't whether it's because of his sexuality,' he says, 'but I don't know if we're seeing the real Wayne. I love him,' he adds, though, rather spoiling the effect. 'I'd fight for Wayne!'

If there are two kinds of drunk, the 'I love you, you're my beshtest mate' drunk and the 'Are you calling my pint a ponce?' drunk, Phil is definitely one the former. In one of the most poignant moments so far the wine causes him to have a near breakdown in front of Linda. A conversation that starts about how he wishes he'd got a little more room in his two-up-two-down in Sutton suddenly gets very deep indeed ...

PHIL: I've got f*** all.

LINDA (joking flirtatiously, trying to defuse the tension): I've gone right off you now.

PHIL (not listening): I've got two little baby girls, which is nice, lovely daughters, and I've got a lovely girlfriend, as well.

LINDA: I know! She'll be there.

PHIL (completely out of the blue): They've taken everything.

LINDA (confused): What?

PHIL: They've taken everything ...

LINDA: What? Who?

PHIL (angrily): Other people!

LINDA: What do you mean 'other people'? Who?

PHIL (mumbles): Don't know. Other people. They've taken all my life.

LINDA (affectionate but exasperated): Who have?

PHIL: Other people!

LINDA: Well they've not taken you.

PHIL (rallying defiantly): No, they haven't. You're damn right they haven't! You're damn right, brother. They ain't taken me. They've tried their f***ing damnedest, though.

LINDA: It's been tough?

PHIL: It has been tough. (Pause.) Not 'tough', tough. But you know …

LINDA: Wearing-you-down tough?

PHIL: I love my Dawny.

LINDA: How long you been with her?

PHIL: Two years. That's why I love my Dawny.

LINDA: Is she there for ever?

PHIL: Yeah. She's there for ever. (Pause.) I just want some 'ever'.

LINDA: You've got it now.

PHIL (tremulously): Hope so.

LINDA (firmly): You know it.

PHIL: Well, yeah, I do know it. I've been wrong before. But I'm not wrong this time. (Desperately) Not wrong this time.

LINDA: Good.

Phil cries, pulls his hat down over his face.

LINDA (heartbroken): Oh, babe!

Meanwhile, Antony is proving himself to be the other kind of drunk. Seeing how much Phil needs a smoke (the cricketer has earlier banged on one of the camera hides, offering £500 for five cigarettes!), he decides to go and get the pair of them some extra supplies. Jo Scarratt, the producer who ended up negotiating with Antony, takes up the story.

'Most of the programme was ready,' she remembers, 'and then suddenly we heard that Antony had gone AWOL, and then that he was at the gate, shouting through it.

'Lou, the safety guy, drove me down and when we got there he had to be my lighting guy, too, covering his torch with a handkerchief! I was met by this bizarre sight of Antony, standing there with a lamp in front of his head, refusing to leave unless I gave him four cigarettes.

'He was climbing up on the fence and Lou was saying, "He's going to break his neck if we're not careful." It became a real safety issue. Then, suddenly, he got down and wandered off and we heard he'd done a runner to the Trial Area. It was pitch black. I didn't have any gaiters, and I was obviously delighted about running after him in there with just Lou and his torch! I'd never even been over the trial bridge before. I'd seen Fash walking over it every day and I wasn't very happy about having to do that myself!

'But we caught up with him on the crow's nest in the middle of the two bridges and now he was refusing to leave unless we gave him two cigarettes for Phil and two for him. I said I was happy to wait all night if I had to and he said he was happy to wait all night too. I did think we might still be there when Ant and Dec came by the next morning!

'Then there was this bizarre turnaround. It had become a real battle of wills. I think he must have sobered up a bit but he didn't want to lose face, so he said, "We're all smelling – give me some eco-friendly deodorant!" So I said we'd give that some consideration. I don't know whether he was so drunk that he thought I'd said that we would actually give him some but he eventually gave in.'

They never did give the celebs the deodorant Antony asked for. Maybe they thought that after that little outburst things would settle down again, but soon it was the producers who were starting to sweat …

Quote of the day

'I just want some "ever".' A tearful Phil breaks hearts across the nation.

Day Seven

Day Seven was tabloid heaven and tabloid hell. The two (and a half) biggest stories of the programme so far broke in a day so action-packed that the entire ITV2 streaming was more exciting than some of the earlier highlights programmes.

The culprits? Exhibit One: a large, brown bush rat. Exhibit Two: a small (very small) portion of popcorn and an even smaller sausage. Exhibit Three: a cosy inflatable seat and a distressed actress unintentionally playing gooseberry.

On another day any one of them could have seized front pages on their own. In the circumstances, the return of Fash to the Trial Area for a record-breaking fourth time was as routine as a day at the office.

'We've got to stop meeting like this,' says a faintly embarrassed Chris Lore.

'Good to see you, Bobbo,' Fash says, nodding familiarly to Bob.

Back in the camp the other celebs are mystified as to why Fash keeps getting voted in. 'Maybe people see him as a hard man with all his martial arts,' says Chris. 'But that's just his way of focusing. He's not showing off. He doesn't even like people watching him. We're all hungry, but he suffers more than any of us 'cos he's got a big frame. I want to appeal to the public, "Leave Fash alone!"'

Even the most inveterate Fash-hater would have to have a grudging respect for the way he takes on the Bobbing For Stars trial. Most people wouldn't even try to retain their dignity while covered in sticky fly pupae, bobbing their head in a box full of leeches for a shiny gold star, or nudging a bemused and sleepy possum out of the way, but Fash not only deals with the creepy-crawlies, he still seems to see himself as the mighty warrior – bringing home the bacon for the team.

What was in the boxes?

1. Fly pupae
2. Meal worms
3. Leeches
4. Rhino beetles
5. Red-claw crayfish
6. Goliath stick insects
7. Orb spiders
8. Rats
9. Eels
10. A mountain brushtail possum

He gets nine stars. Once again, because of Super Fash, the camp won't go hungry. Or so they think. The first intimation that it might not be as easy as that comes after Danniella, in the role of leader, dismissively sweeps aside a snake that the producers had planted on the celebrity chest. A few days ago the celebs would have been in hysterics at the sight of the lugubrious reptile, but now they need a little more hardship to break them. And the producers aren't slow to provide it.

The celebrity-chest question, 'What percentage of people believe in love at first sight: (a) 22 per cent, (b) 64 per cent?' In itself this is a lot more cruel to a group of people who are, they insist, more in love with their respective partners than anyone else has ever been.

They get the question right (64 per cent), but are rewarded only with popcorn.

The paltry reward causes a chain reaction that just keeps growing and growing. 'What a pathetic prize!' Danniella shrieks. 'I'd rather keep the box!'

'Shall we negotiate?' suggests Chris.

'Ask for chilli sauce!' says Toyah. 'Chilli sauce gives the endorphins a boost.'

'We need salt, basically,' offers Chris.

In the production office they're outraged at the celebs' ingratitude. 'You can shove it up your a***!' says the runner responsible for putting together the celebrity chest. 'We've spoiled them! This is supposed to be hard.'

You suspect that the reaction is similar higher up the

command chain. Danniella toddles off to the Bush Telegraph to complain and comes back bizarrely satisfied, at least for a moment. 'They've registered that we're unhappy,' she says.

Registered? What does she think that means? They want you to be unhappy! That's the whole point of the programme.

Maybe not quite as unhappy as Danniella soon becomes, though. Yesterday she came across a huge brown rat, running along the beam in the dunny. Her good mood of Day Five had already started to dissolve and this was almost the last straw. 'I'd rather do six months in Holloway than be in here. I can't do rats,' she sobs, scooping herself a few million more votes from the kindly British public for the 'Rats Crawling Over You and Eating Your Skin' trial.

Today, she's still in an uncertain mood, perhaps because she hasn't peed since last night and doesn't intend to for potentially another week ('I won't be drinking any more water,' she claims).

Later in the afternoon she's called to the Bush Telegraph for an interview and, while the rest of the celebs are away, Chris and Cat (not *The* Cat, that would be a real shock etc. etc.) seize the chance to play.

'Can I sit on there?' Catalina asks coyly, as Chris lounges suavely on his inflatable chair.

'Course you can,' he squeaks.

There'd been rumours, reported in the *People*, that the two of them had already sneaked off to the pool in the middle of the night for an off-camera forty-minute session of, well, something the night before. Philosophical discussion? Crocheting? Let your mind run wild. Unfortunately (or fortunately, depending on how you look at it), no camera was available to follow them.

So, as the pictures go out live on ITV2, the digital nation is alive with millions – well all right thousands – of people trying to remember their Desmond Morris *Naked Ape* shtick. So he's got his leg pointed away from hers. Does that mean he wants to shag her? He has shagged her? Or he just wants a banana?

Things have certainly changed since Catalina told him off like a naughty schoolboy for soaking her with his big water pistol. They're discussing Fash's latest trial ordeal but she's much keener to talk about the nice, cuddly possums than the distinctly unsexy beetles. 'Possums,' she purrs, in a baby voice, 'they're furrrry.'

Just at the point when it looks like Chris might explode, Danniella comes back from the Bush Telegraph, her face taut and uncomfortable.

'I just cried my eyes out in that interview,' she says, bursting into tears all over again. 'I'm sorry, I'm making everyone depressed.'

'You're not making us depressed!' cries Catalina with rare warmth, hugging her friend. 'I love having you here.'

'I feel like a bad mother, walking out and leaving my kids for two weeks, just for a job,' Danniella cries. 'I really can't stand it.'

'You want to go?' says Cat. 'You really want to go? Let's go and talk to them now.'

The two women walk back up the hill towards the Bush Telegraph but, after long discussions with the camp psychiatrist, Sandra, Danniella's persuaded to stay, at least until the first eviction. ('They asked me if it's worth it for a hot meal and a shag,' says Danni. 'I said yeah, it is!')

But for anyone who thought Catalina seemed a little too eager to see her friend go, her reaction afterwards only adds to the confusion. 'I'm really pissed off now,' she tells Linda. 'It makes her look even better now that she has gone back in. The fact that she was about to walk out, everyone is going to say she stayed and she will get, "Good on you for that!" And then, if she walks out, it will look better. It will be like, "She was upset. She stuck it out and she went back. She really wanted to go." But I think it was a bit manipulative.'

An army of paparazzi are now waiting outside the Versace Hotel for Danniella to show up but, in the meantime, an even bigger storm is brewing.

After shrugging off the skanky blue vest of the Chef, Antony Worrall Thompson has at last shocked everyone by pulling on the tight white vest of the Rebel (only in a metaphorical sense, luckily).

Yesterday he tried to blackmail the producers into providing more cigarettes and today he came close to persuading the whole camp to walk out. As you'd expect, the breaking point for our rotund chef was food. Celebrity equations were suddenly confronted with a new one:

Late meal = wild, rebellious, angry celebs

BEHIND THE LENS

One of the producers on *I'm A Celebrity* ..., Jo Scarratt, is a close friend of Danniella Westbrook and she knows more than most about the pressures that made her think about quitting on Day Seven.

'I followed her for five months to make a Channel 4 documentary [*Danniella Westbrook: My Nose And Me*] about her,' Jo explains, 'and we became friends through that. It's weird 'cos before I started filming her I thought I wasn't going to like her at all. But I liked her a lot and we speak to each other every few days now. We had our differences, and she can drive you mad at times, but she's great. When I met her, because she'd just got clean, and she'd just got rid of all her old friends, I think she appreciated the fact that I didn't bullshit her. She'd been surrounded by all these hangers-on but I didn't want anything from her.

'Obviously she knew I'd worked on last year's series and she said, "What do you think?" And I said I thought it would be good for her. The one thing that really annoys her, and it annoys me too, is that people always say, "She's not really clean, is she?" and I know she is. And I thought if she stayed in the jungle for a couple of weeks it would prove to everyone that she is.

'The thing with Danni is that she's got such a strong relationship with Kevin. He's a recovering addict, too, and they're together twenty-four/seven. She's quite an emotional person and I hope people realize that. She really misses her children – Jody B's only eighteen months old.

'She's certainly not acting in there! I think one of the reasons she might want to go is that she doesn't want to be voted out – at least this way she can say she walked out of her own accord.

'If she thought the public hated her that would be a real blow. And she does have a huge rat phobia – seeing that rat will really have freaked her out. But I think she'll regret it if she leaves. She's stuck with it for a week. Why leave now?'

To begin with it all starts as a bit of a joke. Nine of the ten celebs are squeezed into the Bush Telegraph hut (Fash is sleeping off his millionth sit-up of the day) and they're giggling like a bunch of kids larking around in a photo booth.

'I can assure you that food is minutes away,' the producer on duty coos soothingly, but the mood is rapidly changing.

'This is a f***ing joke!' says Antony, suddenly. 'We'll put our heart into this show if we think that you're cooperating, but you're taking the piss. We haven't moaned when we've only got four meals because we know that's the game, but at least have the meals ready on time.

'This is a bloody TV show, not a concentration camp or a prison,' he continues. 'If we all walk out you're screwed. You've got a live show to do!'

By now, of course, the food is arriving back in camp and they dutifully troop back down towards it, but their blood is still up. And the basket, slowly descending on a rope from the sky, looks disappointingly small. 'We've got three mange tout and one sausage each,' says Antony, dismissively tossing the meagre rations aside.

They head back up to the Bush Telegraph hut but this time there are no giggles.

'Nine sausages, I'm sorry, doesn't constitute a meal,' says Antony. 'Nine pieces of cauliflower, 27 mange tout, two mushrooms and four kiwi fruit and some nuts without a nut cracker. What's wrong with you? It's meant to be nine main meals. It's less than a thousand calories a day.'

'I can assure you that the portions are very carefully worked out. The calorific value—'

'F*** the calorific value!' says Antony savagely.

'If he served that in his restaurant for nine people he would be struck off,' Danni adds, perhaps imagining chefs have to take some kind of Hippocratic oath to provide reasonable portions. She's obviously never been to a Little Chef.

'We are sticking together here,' Antony continues. 'You are not going to part us or split us; you are not going to have one faction against the other. We are a unit and we are going together … and … I want to speak to my agent in the morning. But, as I understand it, if we say, "I'm a celebrity … get me out of here!" Then we're out of here.'

They're out of here. In the ultimate symbol of rebellion, they cover the camera and head back across the bridge screaming those fatal words, 'I'm a celebrity … get me out of here!'

Waiting, ready for what turns into tense negotiations, is the series editor Richard Cowles and executive producer, Natalka Znak.

'Natalka and I were watching in the Bush Telegraph as they made their demands,' Richard explains. 'The food had been delayed because of Danniella's antics and when it did arrive they didn't like it, to say the least! I heard Antony say "Turn right!" And at that point Natalka and I sprinted out of the hut because we knew that meant they weren't heading back to camp.

'They were saying "Let's storm the bridge!" Those bridges are only designed to hold five people so we tried to hold them off at the pass but they weren't in the mood to listen to safety advice. Security managed to persuade them to spread out a bit but they were determined to make it up to the studio. We followed them up there and they began to list all their grievances – mainly about the food.

'They get the same portion of rice every day, but they didn't believe me. After a while in camp I think their minds get clouded! On the first day their rice was in a smaller tin so it looked like there was more of it but it was exactly the same. Unfortunately, when I tried to explain that to Antony, he thought I was insulting his chef skills!'

'You're f***ing useless at measuring!' Antony storms, taking a belligerent step towards Richard and looking like he's going to hit him.

'He was never going to hit me!' Richard laughs. 'But I'm not sure that's what everybody thought. Fash and Phil edged across him to provide a human shield – which was quite touching. Apparently they thought I was the nutritionist for some reason, but I don't get involved in the food at all anymore – when I arranged the meals for the stand-ins (the actors who took part in the rehearsal) they all put on weight!'

It's only when the good, reasonable Dr Bob steps in that they begin to calm down. 'You can live on rice and beans for three months without any vitamin deficiency,' he explains.

You can see that they still want to argue but they can't. Bob's a medic. He knows these things.

As they walk away, though, the unity of the group is broken. 'What spoils our argument is the girls begging for pizza,' says Linda.

Antony nods, grimly. The producers have done it again.

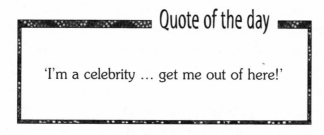

Quote of the day

'I'm a celebrity ... get me out of here!'

Day Eight

Overnight even the weather has turned against our celebs. The camp has been lashed with wind and rain and a soaked Sian ends up having to sleep in the Bush Telegraph hut. What must make it worse is that she knows that all over the country people are saying, 'Why didn't she predict it was gonna rain? Ha-ha-ha-ha!'

The mood is more subdued than yesterday. Fash in particular obviously feels they were a bit harsh towards the poor producers: 'We got the point over a little more forcefully than necessary,' he says, sadly.

On the evening programme the producers show footage of Fash talking honestly and sensitively about his brother Justin and suddenly everyone at home realizes what his fellow celebs have known since the start: he's not such a bad bloke, really.

Antony, though, has got the opposite agenda. For the first time both the producers and one of the celebs are colluding in how they want to be seen. Antony wants to be seen as a villain because he feels sorry for

Fash and wants to take the trial heat off him and, more importantly, because he likes being the centre of attention.

The producers want Antony to be seen as a villain because they really think he *is* a villain (acting as if you were going to punch the person in charge of editing every moment of your day is probably not a good PR move) and because they really, really don't want to see Fash doing yet another trial.

The plan works for both sides. When the votes come in, it's Antony who's sent out to the lake to do battle with Trial Eight: 'What Lies Within?' If it had been Fash doing the trial you'd know that what lay within would be giant killer leeches, jellyfish and scuba divers with chainsaws. Or at the very least he'd have made it look like that.

What lies within for Antony, it turns out, is one deeply bored snake, and a couple of apathetic eels (mysteriously all the crocs seem to have gone on their holidays). He simply wades through the lake, shoves them out of the way by turning the bag he's been given into a sort of oven glove, and grabs the stars hidden in various tubes.

'That was supposed to trap his hand,' says one of the producers sadly, as Antony's 'oven glove' foxes a booby trap in one of the tubes. ('I, Chefman, will defeat your evil plans!') Ultimately, he gets only five stars, but that's just because he can't quite drag himself backwards and forwards across the lake in time.

So Antony has overtaken Fash as the number-one

hero to the others and managed to get a top-secret message to his wife with the legend '143' written on his arm. Apparently, 143 means 'I love you' in text speak, although, since it's only 14-year-olds who speak text fluently, he probably got it wrong and told his wife 'I want bog.'

After the shenanigans of yesterday there's clearly a truce going on between the celebs and their evil captors today. For their part, the producers provide a much nicer celebrity chest (some tea and fondant fancies, very survivalist!) and the celebs endearingly act as if they'd been given a three-course meal. They don't ask for much, you see.

With the first eviction looming, today is also the day when our heroes start to get a little introspective. To facilitate a bit of soul baring, they're invited to the Bush Telegraph to give their views on their fellow celebs; but, as those bits of the interviews were never shown, you'll gather that they were all boringly nice about each other.

Surprisingly, the only slight dig comes from Sian. 'I just didn't know what to say about Chris,' she says as she walks back into the camp. Huh! You try writing a whole book about him.

They're also asked to say why they think people should vote for them. Antony sets his sights far too high by saying, 'I've got to prove I'm not full of bullshit'; as does Chris by promising that he's going to get 'crazier' (as if that were possible!); Fash at last learns some reverse psychology, saying, 'I wouldn't like to be the one left here on their own'; as does Sian, who promises,

'I'm delirious from lack of sleep and I've been bitten all over by mosquitoes'; but Danniella proves she hasn't learned a thing with a simple plea: 'Don't vote for me.' Or was that the greatest reverse psychology of all? Clever!

'I really wish I had done what I was planning to do,' says a doleful Danni later as the afternoon starts to drag. 'But I should give the British public a chance not to vote for me.'

(British public: 'We're confused!')

'In a way it's bit like a bereavement, isn't it?' she also asks, surprisingly not drawing the obvious response from the other celebs: 'Um, no. It's more like *It's a Knockout* in the jungle, Danni.'

Quote of the day

'That was a nice chest, that.' Sian delights innuendo lovers everywhere.

Chris's guide to the trials: Part II

TRIAL FIVE: CATCH A FALLING STAR

Contestant: Danniella

'She was really gung-ho. She had a really great spirit and attitude because the things in those tanks were pretty nasty. We'd originally done it as a Week Two trial, with ten boxes of stuff, but we thought that was a bit too much, so we only used five.

'Box One was actually ultraslime, the stuff they used in *Alien* to make the alien's mouth look really "urrggh!" That stuff makes absolutely everything stick to it. We just called it eel slime! I don't know if you can extract eel slime. I've never tried it but I guess you could – they are pretty slimy!'

TRIAL SIX: THE SNAKE PIT

Contestant: Fash

'My opinion is that Fash is a wonderful con man. He's

conquered three major fears in three trials! When he walked in there, there was a snake above a star on a tree and he just picked [the star] up. He gives good trial, though, you have to say that!

'And it's fun when the celebs talk about it afterwards 'cos they always embellish the details – the snakes become fifty feet big! Fash was saying that they were obviously wild snakes and that we were making them really angry. And that they were obviously hungry!

'That's why snakes attack people!' laughs the associate trials producer 'because they're hungry and they want to eat them!'

'Most of those snakes were about as tame as snakes can get. But there were a couple that were a little more feisty,' Chris continues. 'In fact, we couldn't put them in with the Americans on their show because the producers wouldn't let us. They were already in a state of revolt and a python bite would have been the last straw.'

TRIAL SEVEN: BOBBING FOR STARS

Contestant: Fash

'Great sportsmanship again from Fash. He really went for it. The first thing we had was the ultraslime once again, with fly pupae in it. Everything stuck to him after that.

The worst box was probably the yabbies [crayfish]. Those things could have given him a nasty nip. The stick insects looked great but unfortunately they'd moved away from the star.

'I'd put the golden orb spiders in there about a week before and they spin a web every day, so he came out with web all over him and the rats must have been really bad – he'd have really pooped his pants at that.

'Possums have got really sharp teeth and really sharp claws, but Tonka is the sweetest possum you could ever hope to meet. His mother was hit by a car when he was very small, and he was injured, so he's got a steel pin in his leg, and he was never released into the wild.'

TRIAL EIGHT: WHAT LIES BENEATH?

Contestant: Antony

'I was a little disappointed with that trial. Antony was too good. He wasn't going to put himself out by charging the course. He went round slowly and got the five stars, but the idea is that you charge round and all these things happen to you and it's a real chaotic soup trial.

'Also, the snakes weren't working that day. They were supposed to be sitting on the stars but they'd pushed them to the front and gone to sit in the warm at the back.

'In future I'll make each star a bit harder on this one. Wayne came and played really hard and only got two stars but Antony took it easy and came away with five. I think he was too cool to play our silly game.'

Day Nine

Day Nine was supposed to be the day when the first unfortunate evictee had her or his last moment in the limelight, before being banished to the outer darkness of *GMTV* and *This Morning*.

Unfortunately for Sian, after a week of anonymity (or as close as you can get to anonymity with 30-odd cameras on you) she was not only booted out, but was overshadowed by one of the other celebs again. It seems that Danniella wasn't practising reverse psychology after all. Not that anyone apart from Catalina really thought she was.

As Ant and Dec walk in to give the bad news with their trademark air of deep, deep seriousness, Sian bears up well but in the corner Danniella's face is scrunching into a teary mess.

Later she famously dubbed the British public 'f***ing w****rs!' for voting for her but, to be fair, at least 56 million took the opportunity *not* to vote for her. That's quite an endorsement, Danni! Look out for Tony Blair introducing the same system at the next election.

Luckily Danniella's not so upset that she can't spare a few moments to give a little support to Catalina, who got the second fewest votes. 'It's not a bad thing to be voted *right down*,' she tells her.

When she walks out at last it's almost an anticlimax and you can tell she wants to stretch the last seconds out a little bit. 'Where's my hat?' she cries. 'I can't go without my hat!' They find her hat, she hugs all the others warmly, and then she walks the long walk across the bridge back to reality. Wonder if it'll be quite as great as she remembered?

Meanwhile poor Sian just looks a little hurt and confused. On the one hand she really wants to get out: she's hardly slept for days and she's been savaged by mosquitoes. But, then again, it's not exactly a vote of confidence, is it? What did she do wrong?

How did they do?

SIAN LLOYD: EVICTED — FIRST

'Poor Sian,' says Ant the night before the eviction. 'If she gets voted out tomorrow, she'll be remembered for saying "That's a nice chest, that" and having a greasy face!' Harsh but fair. Sian was probably just a bit too nice. You could see that she wanted to lash out on occasions, but she bit her tongue and, as a result, most shots just showed her smiling brightly, while inside she was undoubtedly swearing like a trooper. Mr Bassey the bear didn't seem to do much, either.

Highest high: Finally managing to 'change her shoes' six long days into camp.

Lowest low: Shivering miserably in the Bush Telegraph hut the night after the mutiny.

Best quote: For giving us some insight into the raging beast within: 'I've reached the stage where I don't care. For f***'s sake, be yourselves.' And this was just on Day Two!

Entertainment value: 2/10. Phil summed it up best: 'She was little Sian-y, wasn't she?' he said breezily. 'She kept talking about cream teas!' Impossible to dislike but not easy to notice.

Niceness: 8/10. Very nice indeed.

All the celebs, with the possible exception of Catalina, seemed sad to see Sian and (especially) Danniella go, but Wayne was particularly devastated. Who would he bitch with now? He and Danniella still seemed to believe that certain – unspecified – members of the group were focused purely on winning and nothing else. Even the way some of the other celebs said 'Good morning' gets on Wayne's nerves. 'They're all full-on!' he snaps. 'It's "Morning!" That's not natural.'

'Let's have a bonding session,' says Antony, drawing them into a big group hug, still blissfully unaware of the fact that another war is brewing – this time between the grumpy owls and the overenthusiastic larks.

Luckily, they've still got Phil – the one member of the group everybody likes. 'Fash is what I'm not,' he'd said earlier in the week, and here's an example, as he takes on his first Bush Tucker trial: the Shooting Star.

Maybe even Fash couldn't have done his trademark kung fu moves in the harness of the Flying Fox, but he'd have at least given us a few of his 'C'mon, Fash!' and a quick 'Focus!' Phil, in contrast, is busy asking Dec about the football, 'How did the Gooners do?' he enquires genially, when he's suddenly sent hurtling, spinning violently, down the rope slide towards the stars at the bottom.

With the misshapen bat in his hand he must know that cricket fans everywhere are making jokes about his batting skills – he had a test average of about seven – but he's about to prove them wrong. With a few lazy stretches he takes out five stars in one run. 'No one's ever done that well,' said the trials supervisor Chris Lore admiringly afterwards.

In his three slides down the Flying Fox he picks up eight of the nine available stars, but you can tell that he's had a lot of practice with excuses after he misses the last one. 'I just twizzled around at the death!' he moans. 'I knew I should've opened a bank! All this bowling lark!'

If we tend to forget that he was actually a pretty good sportsman (albeit only a cricketer), it's because he's so self-deprecating. Later in the day, the celebs are given a bat, a ball and some stumps and Phil gets to do his two favourite things: play cricket and take the mickey out of himself. For once he seems to be showing off, demonstrating the correct stance and way to hold a bat.

'Why did you never do that in test matches?' Antony demands – but Phil hasn't finished.

'… and what usually happens is you look behind you and the wickets are all over the place,' he laughs.

How can the others compete with that? Chris has obviously decided that he's going to make himself a bit more of a character, but it's really not him. After they win ten eggs from the celebrity chest, Antony instructs them all to count out five minutes as a kind of human egg timer. To begin with, it's mildly amusing. Taking it in turns, with Antony conducting, they count, 'One Mississippi, two Mississippi, three Mississippi …'

But, of course, five minutes is a long time and gradually they start trying to make the material interesting. In a particularly excruciating moment Chris starts alternating 'Mississippi' with 'hippopotamus' and trying to make it into a kind of rap. No!

When he's himself it's almost as though a *normal* person had been smuggled into the camp. 'I wonder what's happening in Palestine,' he muses at one point, as though no one had told him that actors are supposed to be vain, self-obsessed monsters.

Luckily for him, though (or not, depending on how you look at it), Catalina is still pinning her hopes on him for her survival. In the day's begging session, when they're asked to say why the public should vote to keep them in, she says, 'Please vote for me 'cos Chris needs looking after.' She doesn't actually nod, or wink, but then she doesn't have to.

Quote of the day

'What do they call them? Fairy fingers?' Wayne struggles to remember what those bits of bread you dip into boiled egg are called. They're called 'soldiers', Wayne. Let's hope he never gets called up.

Mark Durden-Smith
uncovered

Have you ever wished you could be back doing something sensible, like reporting on the rugby?

'Not a bit of it. I haven't done that for about a year. I've had a real sea change since then and this has been an amazing experience – 380 people in the middle of the jungle. It really opens your eyes to the nuts and bolts of making a TV programme. The Australian crew are amazing. We obviously like to hate them because they're so good at everything, but they're really good at this as well.'

What's it like working with Tara?

'It's a nightmare! No, obviously she's a highly unpredictable beast but I wouldn't have it any other way. I've never wanted an easy ride! I wake up every morning thinking, What's she going to throw at me today? She shops like no one else. Every day she comes back and she's got more clothes than I'll ever wear in my entire life. She also wears the shortest skirts that have ever been seen on live TV – that's a real challenge to my professionalism.'

When the mutiny occurred, did you think you might have to spend ten days telling jokes and talking about the weather?

'Ten days talking about myself? I'd have got used to it! I don't think there was ever any real danger of that – they were just getting a bit frisky. What was it Tara said? "I'm ashamed to be British! They're so spoiled." Those sausages actually looked quite nice. Antony was just upset that he couldn't turn them into a nice fricassee.'

You spend an hour a day on the programme. What do you do with the rest of your time?

'I sit around making everybody else's life hell! [ITV2 producer] Michelle writes perfectly good scripts and I go through them and make them average! I do get very involved in it – it's more fun that way and more me.'

Is there anything you've wanted to say and not been able to?

'No, I don't think so. I've got away with saying "knob", "arse", "tits". I haven't wanted to go any further than that because my mother's watching.'

Who did you think was going to win at the start?

'I interviewed them all on the Saturday and Phil had been on a 36-hour bender and he was obviously still a bit pissed. This fly was buzzing around and he said [Mark puts on a woozy voice], "That's obviously a Versace fly." He was really funny and he obviously didn't care about anything, so I thought he'd win.'

Who do you think will win now?
'Phil is obviously still the bookies' favourite but I don't think it's that clear-cut. All of them have got something that will endear them to the public – Antony, Wayne, Toyah, Fash the Bash. It all depends what happens in the next few days.'

Day Ten

Day Ten begins with Ant and Dec deciding to have a little playful fun with our heroes. It has been decided that there'll be no eviction today. Danniella's still the big story and if anyone else is kicked out they'll end up wondering why there are no paparazzi to meet them. And why they have to carry their own bags, hitch a ride to the nearest station, and organize their own flight back to Britain.

But the other celebs don't know that. They're in agony as the Geordies explain that it might be any of them. It's touching to see how desperate they are for just one more day in hell. Catalina even punches the air in triumph when, at last, Ant and Dec let them know that it won't be her – or anyone else.

Meanwhile, on the outside, Danniella is busy proving that everything she said was true – by refusing to sell her story to the highest bidder. The journalists watching the evening programme back at the hotel begin by predicting that she could get up to £250,000 for her story. Gradually, though, as she reveals more and more about what went on in camp, spoiling any possible exclusives, they're busy knocking noughts off until she's left with even less than Sian would get (and even Mr Bassey would get more than Sian).

Nevertheless, Danniella's still as quotable as ever, even if, at times, she sounds as if she's getting her lines from old Celine Dion songs. 'I've been living in a world of hurt,' she croons – I mean says – at one point.

And the AOR disease is obviously catching. 'She's my confidant, and my friend,' says Wayne, almost (but not quite) quoting Andrew Gold's drippy *Golden Girls* theme tune.

How did they do?

DANNIELLA WESTBROOK: RETIRED

Danniella provided some of the most emotional moments of the show with her tears, but on Day Five she gave us a taste of what *could* have been. The happy, feisty, sexy Danniella, who invited Ant and Dec to inspect her 'bristols', made only a brief appearance, but it was enough to see what the other celebs (except Catalina, occasionally) liked so much about her. 'I think she's one of God's beautiful creatures,' said Toyah. 'A proper bird,' added Phil, approvingly. Shame she had to go so soon.

Highest high (no pun intended): Making Day Five's bug shower look like some kind of holistic health treatment.

Lowest low: Discovering a rat in the toilet on Day Six.

Best quote: 'I miss Kevin, and the children – and I miss chocolate!'

Entertainment value: 8/10. If she'd stayed she'd surely have been one of the frontrunners to win.

Niceness: 8/10. Lovable but dappy.

Nevertheless, it's a jungle out there, as Ant and Dec keep reminding us, and life goes on. Like marathon runners coming into the last leg, our celebs are now jostling for advantage in the pack and one or two of them are getting ready to sprint.

For the first seven days, Toyah seemed happy just revelling in the kind of domestic tasks that seem extraordinary when you're a wealthy actress, singer and presenter. 'The public should vote for me 'cos I'm a worker ant. The camp will fall into disarray if I go,' she said on Day Nine, giving the worst manifesto yet. Did she really think people were deciding their vote on the basis of how clean the dishes were?

Today, though, she got the chance to do her first Bush Tucker trial. This was what she'd been waiting for from the beginning, a chance to show her stuff. Literally. Before the series started Toyah said that she was looking forward to getting naked in the jungle, forcing the producers to draw up all sorts of contingency plans for that eventuality (everything from declaring a national emergency to issuing special glasses with little black dots in strategic places).

Trial 10, Tea Time In Hell, looks as if it might provide the opportunity that she'd been waiting for. In a clearing at the Trial Area, Ant and Dec sit primly behind a table piled up with scones and tea, and in front of them a pool of the most vile slime imaginable bubbles and steams revoltingly. Just to add to the charm, Bob is around to explain what else might be in there. 'There'll be maggots,' he explains, 'and possibly leeches. You don't want to go in there with your jeans on,' he adds. 'They'll get disgusting. Are you wearing shorts underneath?'

Toyah's eyes light up and the nation holds its breath.

'I'm just wearing a swimsuit underneath,' she says happily, 'but I don't mind.'

Only someone who's wasted years of their life in the gym can strip off with the confidence that Toyah shows, as she slips out of her outer clothes and into the pool. And that's when it happens. Suddenly, after nine days of saying nothing, Toyah suddenly becomes interesting. And kind of funny.

'It's like a tearoom, isn't it?' offers Ant.

'I've never known a tearoom smell of shit!' she ripostes.

'What does it smell like?' asks Dec, through his gas mask.

'Vegetation, rot, death, decay, *Texas Chainsaw Massacre* – it's hell!' she says, rather too eloquently.

And then, 'I've been in showbiz for twenty-five years – I'm used to grovelling in shit.'

And then, 'I wish I'd plugged up certain orifices.'

And then, stinking appallingly and preparing to head off to camp, 'I wonder if I'll pull on the way back!'

The most amusing moment doesn't make the programme (for obvious reasons). Just like Danniella, she tries to persuade Bob to clean her off but he's having none of it. The producers want to make her walk back to camp like that.

'Bob, you're a c**t,' she says, affectionately, heading back with five of the eight stars.

But apparently she has some experience of dealing with unfortunate smells. Later in the afternoon the celebs are asked to talk about some of the key moments in their life: the best, the worst, the most embarrassing.

At times it gets painfully sad – when Phil and Linda talk about the death of their mothers – but Toyah, quite reasonably, doesn't want to open up that much. Instead, she tells a story about being sewn into her costume on stage in the eighties and having 'the squits'. Fash, who seems to have grown up in a kind of bizarre Enid Blyton novel (*Five Learn To Focus? Five Decapitate the Opposition?*), isn't quite sure what the squits are. 'Runny tummy, you mean?' he asks, sweetly.

Suffice it to say the story ends with Toyah saying, 'And they couldn't get the radio mike off me in time.' Urrggh!

And, once again, Catalina shows us a glimpse of a nicer, more self-aware person within – before stomping on the bitch, ruthlessly. When they're asked about career highlights, Fash talks about playing at Wembley, Chris about winning a BAFTA, Phil about being picked for England, and Catalina says, 'I don't really have a career. This is the highlight of my career!' A rather endearing quote. But then of course she immediately backtracks and starts going on about how she's got 'lots of careers'.

Silly girl. Mind you, you have to respect her brazenness. Having only yesterday berated Danniella for trying the old reverse-psychology trick, today she decides to try it herself. 'I hate it here now,' she pouts, tossing her hair and practically blowing air kisses to the camera. 'Please can you vote me out?'

The British public aren't that stupid, are they?

Catalina is also eager to let the other celebs know a bit more about Danniella. 'She's got a bodyguard out there,' she says coyly.

'Has she?' asks a surprised Phil.

Cat nods, tight lipped.

'Has she?' asks Toyah, even more surprised.

Cat nods again in an I'm-not-being-bitchy-'cos-I'm-not-actually-saying-anything kind of way.

Luckily, Fash is available to come to Danniella's defence. 'It's more for her own protection than anything else,' he explains, helpfully.

There was more bitching to come when Linda and Catalina decided to make a 'daring' break for the bridge. Unfortunately, when they got there, they weren't exactly sure what to do. 'We're negotiating,' announces Catalina, missing the point that last time the celebs won a small victory because the producers were scared that the whole programme was going to fall apart. This time they're just scared that the bridge might fall apart. As a result, they don't let anyone else on, so Cat and Linda are left there on their own looking silly.

'Shall we go back?' says Catalina eventually, in a small voice.

Of course, when they get back, they describe it as a kind of Mexican stand-off, but it's more like a Belgian or a Swedish stand-off. ('We shall not be moved!' 'You're being unreasonable.' 'Sorry for bothering you, officer.')

But the others aren't terribly impressed. Fash lets rip with the most violent swearword in his vocabulary. 'It was undisciplined,' he sighs.

'It smacks of desperation,' Antony adds, slightly hurt that the lovely Linda has thrown in her lot with bad old Cat.

The idea that Antony, Linda and Phil are a team within the team – the three musketeers – started as a bit of a joke, but now members of both factions seem to be taking it too seriously.

For the first time, the unthinkable happens and someone even bitches slightly about Phil. 'He wants it desperately. He's really working for it,' says Wayne.

There's a brief shocked silence from Antony and Fash.

'I don't see that,' says Antony, politely, at last.

'Phil is exactly as he is,' says Fash. 'He's not trying anything!'

But you can see that Wayne and Catalina feel a little left out, and they'd like to form a new clique of their own. Unfortunately, the only noncombatant, Chris, is having none of it. Nobly resisting Catalina's attempts to make him slag off the other celebs, he says, 'Just because the three of them are mates and they drink doesn't mean they're a clique. I get on with them all individually. I don't care, anyway. You're mistaking me for someone who gives a shit!'

What a nice man. Surely he must be favourite to win now.

Not if Catalina has her way. She's decided on a new strategy. 'Please vote for me,' she says, bizarrely changing her tune. 'I love it here! The others all want to see their families and I don't, so you'd be doing everyone a really big favour by voting for me.'

Surely the British public aren't … well, whatever Danniella said!

Quote of the day

'I walked out on what was at the time a lot of money: a hundred thousand pounds.' Antony describes his toughest career moment with the modesty he's famous for.

Day Eleven

'The British public have decided that the person they want out is … Chris,' Ant and Dec announce on the eleventh day, but, for the first time, they're wrong. It wasn't that the British public wanted Chris *out*: they just weren't all that bothered about his *staying in*.

He'd been rather stitched up by all the other celebs. Belatedly realising that the Bush Tucker trials are their show reel, they'd all seized the chance to demonstrate how brave, game and witty they could be with insects gnawing their skull and so forth, while assuring poor old Chris that he'd get his chance later.

He never did. There's a brief moment of shock when he hears the news, a quick shrug and he's off across the bridge to meet his mum. Maybe Catalina's ploy succeeded, or perhaps she was helped by the Catalina-oils-her-firm-flesh montage that the producers helpfully put together for the programme.

And perhaps her fans forgot that, if they wanted to see her in 'action', they needed someone for her to be in action with.

How did they do?

CHRIS BISSON: EVICTED — SECOND

Danniella was surprised to hear that Chris was considered the quiet one of the group. 'He's not quiet,' she insisted in her first interview. 'People think actors are boring, but he's a funny bloke.'

It's true that he joined in all the camp banter, and he was probably the only celeb who got on equally well with every single person, but nothing he said was ever quite funny or controversial enough to make the show. It's not even that he was boring. If he *had* been, there'd have been clips of him sending the others into a coma – stifled yawns and what have you. No, unfortunately, he wasn't quite as interesting as that.

Highest high: Soaking Catalina on Day Four.

Lowest low: Being sent flying by the exploding spider on Day One (he later claimed this was because Antony knocked him over by jumping out of the way).

Best quote: 'We'd be snookered without Antony' or 'I want to say to the public, "Leave Fash alone"' or even, most heroically, 'I get on well with Cat.'

Entertainment value: 2/10. One point for the inflatable seat, the most sensible luxury item, and one for the super-soaker, the most entertaining luxury item.

Niceness: 10/10. Impossibly loyal and nice to everyone.

Meanwhile, bits were starting to fall off the rest of the celebs. Antony injured his back abseiling up a waterfall to get the Celebrity Chest on Day Ten (naturally he told the others he'd done it rescuing Elle McPherson from a gang of ravenous kangaroos) and he was starting to feel the pinch.

'I'm not sure my back will last out,' he said. 'Depending on the vote tomorrow I may be Casualty Number Two after Danniella – I'm not quite sure that I can keep going.' Unfortunately, because of the complexities of celebrity speak, it was impossible to work out whether this meant he wanted to go or wanted to stay.

Elsewhere in the camp they were all pretty sure that they wanted to stay. Fash, never one to use celebrity niceties, put it best: 'The bottom line is, it's a competition and we all want to win.'

But could it be possible that subconsciously they're doing all they can to escape? Even to the extent of trying to get themselves invalided out?

Wayne is bouncing balletically on his bed when suddenly he plummets through the flimsy material and onto the ground below.

'Wayne!' says Fash, rushing maternally to his assistance. 'Oh, goodness!'

'What happened?' says Toyah.

'Wayne was trampolining and he fell through.'

'I was not!' Wayne fibs shamelessly, trying to think of a more dignified explanation ('I saw a spider on my bed and I was trying to stamp on it and … and …') but he's forced to give up. 'Shut up, Fash!' he snaps.

Fash smiles ruefully. He's learned by now that some of the celebs are a little weaker than he. Sometimes the Fash must know when to turn the other cheek.

'Footballers get the same injuries,' he explains later, 'but he's a ballet dancer and they do need a lot more attention and hugs and kisses.'

More hugs and kisses than a footballer? Anyone who watches *The Premiership* will know that he's talking about unimaginable obscenity!

But, then again, the other celebs are becoming concerned about Fash's mental health. His titanic exercise regime has at last taken its toll and he's pulled a hamstring: a cue, naturally, for him to work even harder, carrying a knapsack full of rocks around with him at all times.

In a further sign that the camp's going stir-crazy, the celebs are becoming increasingly obsessed with the disembodied voice they speak to every day, their only link with the outside world. By coincidence, the two main scanner operators, Rebecca De Young and Luisa Diaz, have similarly honeyed tones and the celebs refer to them as 'Cadbury Girl' and 'Voice-y'.

Phil visibly melts when he hears those magic words – 'Can Fash please make his way to the Bush Telegraph?' – echoing out over the intercom.

'That's my Voice-y,' he sighs. 'That's the voice that does it for me!'

Catalina's not impressed. 'Someone like Mariella Frostrupp's got a really sexy, husky voice,' she argues.

'Yeah,' agrees Phil dreamily, 'but so's Voice-y. She's in my top five!'

'Do you know why men find a husky voice sexy?' asks Linda who, it's been noted, seems to be something of an expert on these matters. 'It's because a husky voice means your larynx is partially closed, which is very similar to when you orgasm!'

BEHIND THE LENS

Luisa 'Voice-y' Diaz (control-room producer and 'Voice of God'): 'I try to sound nice and soothing because the Voice of God is somebody who looks after all their wants and needs. You're the only person from the production team that they talk to and they do start getting interested in what you're like. They say, "What's your name? Where do you come from? Do you have a boyfriend?"

'While you're in there, these things are important to them because they've got nothing else to think about, but as soon as they're out they'll probably forget all about it. Phil comes in sometimes and says, "I'm bored – can I just have a chat?" and they've all said, "Don't I know you from somewhere?" They think they know me, but I've never met any of them before!

'When they're hungry they can get a bit snappy and after the mutiny they apologized 'cos they swore at me. They shouted up, "Sorry Voice-y!" '

But then, of course, we've already seen the celebs obsessing about their food and their shelter. It's only natural that sex will be next. After they get the day's celebrity-chest question right ('Who won the Premiership – Manchester United or Arsenal?') and are rewarded with a large hit of ice cream, their libidos seem to go into overdrive.

Well, apart from Wayne, who's still being a martyr after his earlier injury. 'I do like ice cream,' he says, tossing his remaining hair in a Catalina style. 'But I just want you all to enjoy it.'

That's not going to be a problem. 'It's like an Ann Summers party,' whispers Toyah to Linda as she turns the box upside down to lick any remaining ice cream out of the corners. Luckily, Fash doesn't hear her. Like most of us, he'd probably been told that Ann Summers parties were just about selling lingerie and, uh, stuff.

'What a nice treat!' he announces brightly, in full-on Mary Poppins mode.

Even before the ice cream arrived Linda had already, like Danniella before her, seized on the Bush Tucker trial as an opportunity to sexually harass Ant and Dec. Not that they seemed to be complaining.

Despite the fact that she's lost a lot of weight in the last ten days ('These cheekbones will look great with a bit of makeup,' she exults over her new, ultra-chiselled profile), Linda still looks fantastic and she practically bounces her way down to the Trial Area for Terror in the Trees.

'The guys have said don't trust Ant and Dec!' she

warns them with a dangerous sparkle in her eyes.

'We're impartial,' protests Dec.

'Yeah,' says Ant, momentarily forgetting what 'impartial' means in all the excitement. 'We're on your side.'

You get the feeling that Ant and Dec would happily shin up the tree for her, particularly when she's trying to get her legs into the harness. 'I'm verging on the obscene,' she giggles. But she doesn't need any help. After ten days in the jungle, the little beasties covering the stars aren't all that terrifying at all. 'Be careful of the huntsman spiders,' warns Ant. 'They're the fastest spiders in Australia.'

Fastest! You're going to need to find a scarier superlative than that. This isn't Sports Day. If they can't rot your flesh with a single bite, then we're not really interested.

She zooms up the tree, chucks the stars down with barely a qualm, zooms back down, gives Ant and Dec a quick snog and then shoots back to camp.

'She can do more trials,' says Dec happily.

By the time the celebs get to consume the results of her hard work, even Fash seems to be getting a little frisky. Despite the fact that the producers have prevented Antony from doing all the cooking, he's still performing miracles, plucking and chopping a straggly chicken, and Fash is very impressed indeed. 'I don't even want to eat it,' he groans. 'I just want to look at it and smell it. Let me take it to bed.'

What would Mrs Fash think?

Predictably, though, not everyone's happy. Catalina doesn't like the way Antony's chopping the chicken. Or the way he throws the rubbish in the fire. Or something.

'A row. How exciting!' says Antony with bleak sarcasm. He doesn't seem to be having much fun any more.

Catalina pouts.

'Are you OK?' Linda asks her solicitously.

'No, I'm not OK,' she spits. 'I'm going to kill someone in a minute.'

She doesn't of course. Eventually, she stops sulking and eats some of Antony's chicken – even making an apology of sorts.

But Antony is still in a glum mood and, later on, he and Phil have another of those wine-fuelled philosophical conversations.

It begins with the least plausible escape plan yet. 'I might put my coat on tomorrow if I'm not voted out,' Antony ponders. 'They're not used to me like that. I reckon you could breeze through the building and out the other side, as long as you're blasé about it.'

To which you have to say, um, 'What building, Antony?'

Phil is confused, too. 'Do a runner, you mean?' he asks. 'You can't do a runner now – that'd be stupid.'

But Phil is perfectly happy to leave when his time comes, too. 'If all you're doing is hanging on to win it, what's the point of that?' he asks. 'There's nothing to win.'

'King of the jungle?' Antony offers wryly. 'A nice big contract from the newspapers?'

'What's that?' asks Phil. 'A fat pain in the arse. I've

'**WELCOME TO THE JUNGLE**' Ant and Dec wait for the next celebrity to arrive for the Bush Tucker Trial.

THE FASH! Fighting snakes… braving insects… swinging over great heights
Nothing scares the jungle's very own Superhero.

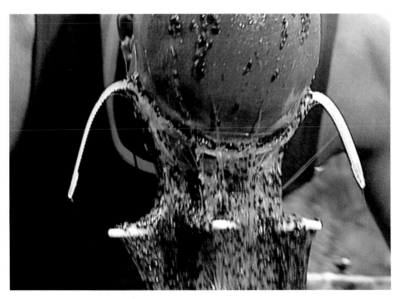

Crocs don't scare Catalina, in fact, she's angling for a specially made pair of crocodile shoes and the crocs are staying out of the way.

A real hero: despite his horrific task, Wayne didn't complain and didn't try to exaggerate the trial as an excuse for his failure (although it would have been justified).

'They're all in me bristols, look!' Danniella gives Ant & Dec the opportunity of a lifetime. And Phil is more than happy to help clean up the mess.

ARE YOU HAVING FUN YET? Antony and Phil get tough in the jungle. Meanwhile Sian shows her playful side and Fash and Wayne have a heart-to-heart. Things seem to be getting just a little too cosy.

MUTINY! Don't be fooled by all that caring and sharing, Cat's gesture says it all: the celebs are NOT happy. Things take a serious turn when, driven by hunger and led by that well-known anarchist Antony Worrall Thompson, the group rebels and a cry goes up around the camp: I'M A **CELEBRITY GET ME OUT OF HERE!**

learned quite a few things in here. I've got some free therapy off that Sandra bird. The trouble with my game, it's a bit like Geoff Hurst. Everyone goes up to Geoff Hurst and goes, "Hello. Geoff, I remember 1966 when you scored a hat-trick." You're always remembered for what you were rather than what you are.'

If nothing else, Phil can guarantee that he'll be remembered for something else now.

Quote of the day

'I don't think I'll ever work for the British government!' Phil is amused to discover that Fash is a Nigerian diplomat.

Day Twelve

If there's been one big loser from *I'm A Celebrity* … it must be Elizabeth Arden, who make eight-hour cream. After Sian left, the celebrities had more to share out between them, and Catalina, as if knowing she didn't have much time, seemed to put more and more on every day. On Day Twelve, though, when her face had reached crazy, almost Sian levels of shininess, it was her time to go.

'Yes!' she cries unconvincingly when Ant and Dec announce the news. Somewhere outside, you can hear teams of make-up artists gathering their trowels ready to scrape the gunk off.

Actually, it's possible that Catalina genuinely was happy to go by then. The bit the celebs seem to find hardest is having their fate in the hands of the capricious public. And she'd had enough of being stuck with what she called the 'middle-aged' celebs who were left after Chris and Danniella were evicted. Sometimes it seems that she's the only person who believes she's 24.

'It was really *boooring,*' she grizzles to Ant and Dec when she gets out. 'They're all so bossy!'

How did they do?

CATALINA GUIRADO: EVICTED – THIRD

Poor old Catalina. 'No one in England likes me,' she sobbed at one point, increasing suspicions that the celebs must have some secret radio tuned to the outside world. She'd never shown any sign of being that self-aware before and, until she went into the jungle, hardly anyone in Britain had even heard of her. She's come out of the series with her profile massively increased. A situation that she must bitterly regret, given her decision to retire from the celebrity game.

Highest high: Braving the crocodile pit to be the only celeb to win the maximum ten stars. Or, possibly, her 'night of passion' with Chris by the pool.

Lowest low: Suffering a severe sense-of-humour failure when Chris got her with the super-soaker. Or, possibly, her 'night of passion' with Chris by the pool.

Best quote: 'I don't really have a career. This is the highlight of my career!'

Entertainment value: 7/10. Whenever this year's series was in danger of turning into *The Waltons*, you could rely on Catalina to spit in the cherry bowl. Sulky, cynical, vain and self-obsessed, she had a job to do and she did it very well. The producers must love her even if no one else does.

Niceness: 3/10. If *I'm A Celebrity* ... were a pantomime, Catalina would have been the celeb you'd boo and hiss. Underneath it all she's probably very nice.

After Catalina's exit, the celebs left inside are determined to come across as nice, charming individuals – whatever the provocation. One of the programme rules is that at least four people have to remain in camp at all times, and so, when Linda decides to go and watch Fash exercise, the rest of them aren't able to leave, and by now Fash's exercise regime goes on for a very long time indeed.

Back at camp, the hours drag. 'I don't think he likes her watching him exercise,' Antony comments after a while, always a little restless if anyone takes Lindy away.

'Doesn't he?' smirks Wayne.

Linda and Fash are certainly getting on well now. Fash has particularly charmed her by, for the first time, admitting to a little human weakness. 'It's nice to have a cuddle,' he admits.

'Do you want one now?' Linda asks, hurling herself at him before he has a chance to change his mind.

'He was so appreciative. He was getting so much from it,' she melts afterwards. And she seems to get just as much from watching a bare-chested Fash pounding his makeshift punch bag.

The time flies for both of them, but when they finally arrive back in camp – although the others are clearly annoyed – the most vicious comment to come out is a flat, 'Oh, you're back,' from Wayne.

'You'll have to cut your routine back to an hour in future,' Antony tells Fash, reasonably.

'Yes,' Fash agrees, even more reasonably. (Somewhere in the distance, that ripping sound is the producers tearing their hair out.)

But, even if they didn't want to cause a scene (very British), most of them are equally determined to win. 'I really want to win *Get Me Out Of Here ... I'm A Celebrity*,' announces Fash, raising the possibility that his agent had somehow booked him on the wrong show. His version would probably have been a cross between *World's Strongest Man* and *Third Term at Malory Towers*.

It's been Fash's bad luck that he didn't get to do any of the sportier, more physical trials. By coincidence, it was the camp's other sportsman, Phil, who took both the exciting Shooting Star and today's (much tougher) Jungle Slide. And he didn't seem that pleased at all.

'Tuffers isn't there today,' says Fash, perceptively, perhaps hoping that the public will evict Phil on a sympathy vote. 'That's not the old Tuffers: he looked physically and mentally tired.'

Even before he gets to the Trial Area, Phil is panting hard. 'I should've given up smoking,' he admits, probably making Middlesex Cricket Club's selectors feel somewhat less aggrieved that he wouldn't sign another contract with them. All of the celebs have been affected physically by their eleven days in the jungle, but Phil looks as if he's about to collapse.

For the slide, he has to strap himself into a kind of giant elastic band and run forward to grab stars, before the elastic hauls him wearily through a pool of the famous 'eel slime', slithering back to where he started. You get the feeling that the celebs might see that as a metaphor for the whole programme.

Phil manages to get four of the six stars but even missing out on two meals seems like a bit of a blow for the rest of them at this stage. Luckily, the producers have thought of an ingenious way to raise morale. When Danniella left there was much speculation about whether a new celebrity would be introduced to take her place and at last, after protracted contract wrangles, he appears – Colin the Crayfish!

Antony caught the unfortunate crustacean down by the pool (he told the others that Kylie gave it to him in exchange for a quick snog), and initially it seems as if Colin may be the answer to their latest dietary crisis.

'If dinner's rubbish I'm going to eat it,' Linda threatens, in a strange premonition of a possible Series Ten, when the producers will no doubt replace eviction with cannibalism for unpopular celebs.

'No, you're not,' says Wayne. 'I'll go on a starvation diet!'

There's another Belgian Stand-Off before they all agree that little Colin is far too lovable to eat, what with his cute little claws and his shiny little shell. As we've already seen, boredom is more of a problem for the celebs than starvation, and so they're very soon trying to get Colin to entertain them by putting things in his claws.

At last, just as Colin's starting to wonder whether being eaten might not have been preferable, they let him go. 'Was that Tuffers? Have I just met Tuffers?' Toyah says, supposedly voicing Colin's thoughts. It's more likely he's thinking, 'I may not be a celebrity … but get me out of here, anyway!'

Quote of the day

'Don't people realize that when you come out you'll see those tapes and think, What a two-faced pig!?' Catalina tells it like it is.

Chris's guide to the trials: Part III

TRIAL NINE: THE SHOOTING STAR

Contestant: Phil

'That's the perfect trial for a cricketer! For anyone who doesn't have a fear of heights and is mildly athletic, that's gonna be great fun.

'I did wonder if I'd made it too easy when he got five stars on the first run – that's really good! If it had been someone else we'd probably have made the stars nearer – some of the stars were a real stretch but he managed to nick them.

'I was thinking, Hopefully, the fireworks will distract him, otherwise he won't even need the last go. And luckily they did – but he still got eight of the stars.'

TRIAL TEN: TEATIME IN HELL

Contestant: Toyah

'Toyah was great. Right from the start she was fun to

watch. She was being really funny and Ant and Dec were totally grossed out. We didn't even know if she was going to do it, but she didn't hesitate and that pool was disgusting. After working on it I went home and I could still smell it for days.

'We'd had blood and bone in there for a couple of weeks; then we put the ultraslime in again – that's our favourite thing now, with fly pupae in it. And, just in case that didn't stink enough, we had airlines going into it blowing garlic and sulphur – that's why it was bubbling.

'I didn't have a sense of Toyah before that from watching the shows, but she really surprised me. She was sharp and funny and I think that trial kept her in for a couple of days.'

TRIAL ELEVEN: TERROR IN THE TREES

Contestant: Linda

'That's another one that was great in the US show. The guy was terrified of spiders and he absolutely screamed, but Linda just did it. She seemed very focused. She really turns it on, has fun with the guys [Ant and Dec] and then, as soon as I was explaining the rules, she was really focused again. I get the impression that not much fazes her.

'She said beforehand that she didn't like spiders, but the spiders didn't even slow her down. Thank God the bees slowed her slightly! What I really want to do is generate stories for when they go back into camp – something for them to react to and talk about – like Toyah going back covered in shit. But Linda beat us!'

TRIAL TWELVE: JUNGLE SLIDE

Contestant: Phil

'I thought Phil did really well. We wore him out a bit before the start by walking him a long way round, not because we were *trying* to wear him out, but because it was the only way to avoid his seeing it too soon.

'This was another trial where the animals didn't come to work. We had a boxful of pigeons that were supposed to fly up into the air when he came near them, but there must have been a hawk or something around because they didn't come out of the box. The snakes just sat there. The eels just sat there! They all worked when we were practising it – but that's what they say: never work with kids and animals.'

Ant and Dec Reveal All

How does this year compare with last year?

Dec: 'For us it's just got easier. People don't realize what a huge operation it is, doing a nightly OB [outside broadcast] from the other side of the world. For the first show everyone was just learning what worked best but now it runs like clockwork.'

Ant: 'The celebrities have been a lot more media-savvy this time. They seemed aware of the cameras much longer. Last year they seemed to forget the cameras were there after about a day and they immediately started arguing – not realizing what it would look like. This time they've decided to stick together and decided to turn, not against us, but against the programme.'

'The guys have told me not to trust you,' Linda said. Were you hurt?

Ant: 'I was more surprised than anything. We haven't tried to stitch them up or anything like that at all. We try to be impartial.'

Dec: 'We're almost like the ringmasters. If they do something funny, we'll say something about it afterwards, but we try not to be malicious. We wouldn't say anything that we couldn't say to their face because we know that we'll meet them later!'

Do you believe Antony's stories now? Now he's proved himself to be a rebel leader?

Ant: 'I'm not saying he's lying! I'm just really interested. He was in prison in Morocco; he ran away with a tramp. He's got some amazing stories! Especially the one about running away with the tramp. I want to know how that happened. Who made the first move? Did the tramp suggest running away together to him, or was it the other way round? I can't wait till he gets out and I can ask him.'

To the celebrities it's a tough, noble voyage of discovery but to viewers at home it's more like *It's a Knockout* in the jungle …

Dec: 'I know! You've got to have that sense of reality. To them it is really serious. It's hilarious watching Fash doing tai chi with a tree, but you know that that's what gets him through the day. It's hilarious watching Wayne Sleep crawling through the Rat Run with waffles tied to his head, but by that stage they were really hungry and it was important to him to try to win the meals. When he sees that on TV later he'll probably laugh his head off. That whole mutiny was about sausages! That's hilarious! But to them it's a meal – it's life and death.'

Ant: 'What's nice about the programme is that you get to see people you know really well from TV conquering their fears, with that layer of celebrity stripped away.'

After the mutiny did you think you might have to spend ten days telling jokes and acting out scenes from *Byker Grove*?

Dec: 'Up until that point I hadn't thought about that. What if they don't come back? What if they all decided two days into it, "Actually, I don't fancy this much – I'm a celebrity … get me out of here!"?'

Were you given a contingency plan for if that happened?

Dec: 'No. I don't think they could have let that happen. They'd have to have secret pizzas or something delivered!'

Have you ever thought any of the trials were a bit too cruel?

Ant: 'You realize watching them crossing the bridge how hard it is – waiting on the other side for them to get to you. But I don't think any of them have been too hard. I'd find dealing with the spiders difficult – that's my phobia.'

Dec: 'I think we've been on the right side of cruel! The Wheel of Horror could have been pretty nasty but I think Linda got away with it.'

Culture Minister Tessa Jowell has denounced the programme for being exploitative …

Ant: 'I think she's got it wrong. All these people know

what they're getting into and it's just entertainment. Danniella proved that if it gets too much they can just walk out.'

In twenty years' time, if you haven't worked for nineteen years and eleven months, would you go on?

Ant (firmly): 'No.'

Dec (even more firmly): 'No. By then the trials will have got even worse! I've got a lot of respect for them doing it. They're making a lot of money for charity and you can't slag them off – but I couldn't do it.'

Day Thirteen

Day Thirteen was when, with a rude jolt, the more laid-back members of the camp suddenly realized that they were in a competition. It happened to Toyah first, when Ant and Dec announced that she was the latest evictee. Her impressive Bush Tucker trial had bought her a couple more days but she'd never quite made it as one of the big characters of the programme.

How did they do?

TOYAH WILLCOX

For the first week, Toyah was frustratingly dull. She washed up, cleaned the camp and seemed to see it as more of an outward-bound course than a TV show. Many of the production crew who interviewed her said that she was their favourite celeb, much funnier and more entertaining than she came across on screen. When the voting started she suddenly switched it on for the viewers, but too late.

Highest high: Wading through the cesspool for Teatime in Hell.

Lowest low: Arriving back in camp after Teatime in Hell and waiting for the boys to clean her off as they did for Danniella. Strangely, there were no volunteers.

Best quote: 'I've been in showbiz for twenty-five years – I'm used to grovelling in shit.'

Entertainment value: 6/10. Some funny lines.

Niceness: 7/10. At times she seemed as if she were in her own little world, but she provided a crucial shoulder for Wayne to cry on after Danniella left, and she didn't have a bad word to say about anyone.

The camp missed Toyah after she was voted out. When asked the day before who he wanted to see go, Phil randomly chose Toyah, only to change his mind later. 'She's too good at washing up!' he laughed.

But, if they'd heard what she said in her post-eviction interview with Ant and Dec, they might have been quite relieved to see her go. 'I was going to see if I could barter a streak for something,' she told them. 'But Fash stepped in and said, "Toyah, is that really necessary?"'

Hurrah! Go, Fash! And so on…

Meanwhile, back in camp, Phil is getting seriously disillusioned as he realizes that the remaining celebs aren't the great bunch of mates he'd thought they were.

It starts with a seemingly innocuous comment from Linda, revelling in the fact that she's the last girl in camp. 'You'd better get in touch with your feminine side, boys,' she giggles. 'Obviously not you, Wayne.'

Wayne's not amused by the insinuation that he's not a real man. 'What do you mean by that?' he asks stiffly.

'You're in touch, baby!' she says quickly, trying to smooth things over.

Wayne still isn't happy, probably adding Linda's very mild faux pas to a large pile of similar remarks he's had to put up with in his career. As someone whose job involves breaking bones and tearing ligaments on a regular basis, he's obviously a little sensitive about suggestions that he's some kind of sissy.

Over the last few days since Danniella left, he's become increasingly bored and alienated and this is the moment when the bitterness spills out. He starts by laying into 'the homophobic world of football and cricket', but, possibly remembering that's a little close to home for Fash, he turns on Phil: 'Cricket's really homophobic, isn't it?'

Phil says nothing, glowering angrily at his shoes. Later he claims that Wayne 'f****n' called me a bigot', which isn't strictly true, but Wayne had obviously decided it was time to stir up a heated debate. Unfortunately, none is forthcoming. Instead, Phil goes into a long melancholy sulk. 'He's my little mate,' he mutters. 'He f****n' kicked me in the bollocks. I just feel a bit upset, that's all.'

Even his cohorts in the so-called 'terrible trio' aren't immune from his dark mood. He says in an interview that 'a few of them are getting more competitive', and, obviously, as there are only four other celebs left, and 'few' generally means 'more than three, fewer than ten', he's not leaving many of them out.

Linda's certainly becoming competitive. In her own way she's much more focused than Fash and she proves it again with another flawless Bush Tucker trial: perhaps the most skin-crawling yet – the Wheel of Horror. (It was originally called the Wheel of Death – maybe they got the people who changed 'Windscale' to 'Sellafield' in to do a rebranding.)

Actually, there are two wheels of horror. On one of them are pictures of various nasty creatures: snakes, eels, rats, cockroaches and so on; and on the other there are ways of carrying them. The 'ways of carrying them', though, include ways you'd normally use only in a particularly frenzied session of *Supermarket Sweep*: mouth, head, shirt, pants etc.

Anyway, superwoman Linda looks slightly disgusted for about a quarter of a second when Chris Lore is explaining the best way to carry a cockroach in your mouth. ("Butt first", apparently. Put them in the other way and they might try to escape in the wrong direction.) But then she immediately goes to work in her characteristically unflappable way.

Even the creatures seem to appreciate her calm manner. The snake turns its head to look at her as she carries it through the jungle. ('Hey, aren't you that wossername off the telly? No, don't tell me, I'll get it in a minute. Lowri Turner?') But she quickly turns it around, and the rat that she carries in her pants looks positively comfortable. Ironically, the rat that she ends up carrying in her hands gets the worse deal: "Ooh, it's pooing" she complains, a little harshly, as she's holding it by its tail at the time.

Linda's wheel of fortune

Cockroach in the shirt (uses the bottom of her shirt to pick it up and carry)

Rat by hand

Snake by hand

Cockroach in pants (a large pair of white Y-fronts produced by Ant – 'You need a personal shopper,' she declares)

Rat in pants.

In true sitcom fashion, while the one remaining girl's out being sensible and bringing home the bacon (all five stars), the boys are enjoying Laurel-and-Hardy-style pratfalls. Every day, two celebs are chosen to go out and look for the celebrity chest, and this time it's Phil and Antony's turn.

They find the chest reasonably quickly, following a trail of pictures of the other celebs. But when they get there Antony is spectacularly hoisted into the air in a giant net.

'Tommo!' squawks Phil, with his unique gift for referring to everybody by about five different names. That may be why he sometimes seems a little vague – it must be hard to keep track.

While Antony is suspended gently in the air, it's Phil's job to look for the key to the chest, much to the amusement and frustration of the camera crew, who can see exactly where it is.

'In the end he just sat down and said, "Well, I don't know where it is!"' laughs one of them. 'And we were all pointing to it going [mouths] "There!"'

When they get the chest back to camp, the question inside seems to be tailor-made for the group:

According to a recent survey, what percentage of married people say that given their experience they wouldn't get married again?

12%

27%

Our celebs would be justified in regarding themselves as experts in marriage. Phil and Antony alone have been married five times between them. Unfortunately, this seems to bias their answer. 'I get married all the time!' admits Phil. In their current, lonely and romantic state of mind, none of them can imagine that anyone wouldn't want to be married and they plump incorrectly for 12 per cent.

Later that evening, their lovesickness is given a further boost when they're allowed to receive letters from their partners. Wayne has already gone to bed but the remaining four read one another's letters aloud and Linda, in particular, can't control her tears. At that point you can see they all wish that they were out, but you have to remember that they're celebrities, not normal people.

When the time comes to make their daily plea to the voting public they have various different arguments, but they all boil down to the same thing: this is horrible, this is hell, I can't stand it any more, please, please vote for me to stay.

Quote of the day

'You're gross people, you really are.'
Linda learns the best way to carry a cockroach in her mouth.

BEHIND THE LENS

Natalka Znak: series producer

According to Catalina, you carefully spliced the tapes and made her into a pouting cartoon character …

'We just show people as they are. They're all interesting enough that we don't have to do that. Casting's the most important thing and we got a very interesting, very different group of people this time. I don't think anyone really believes that we made Catalina into that character! Also, we have the streaming, so people can see what the celebrities are really like for themselves.'

How does this year compare to last year?

'They're both very interesting and both very different. There was less shouting this year but there have been a lot of revelations. This was a very thoughtful group and I think they got a lot out of it. Antony said, "It was an incredible experience and I learned a lot." I love all of them. I have a lot of respect for them and the way they've opened up. That's why I wouldn't try to distort the way they're seen. I've got too much respect for them.'

Did you think Danniella was right to leave?

'It's up to them: they're all free agents. But I'm glad she stayed until after the first eviction so she could see that the public supported her. It would have been a shame if she'd left without knowing that. But we don't need to keep people in! If they want to leave they can leave.'

When the mutiny happened, did you have a contingency plan for if they'd all walked out for good?

'No. I was just relying on my powers of persuasion. I honestly don't know what we'd have done if they'd decided to go. I didn't even think that they'd walk out as far as they did – me and Richard [series editor] had to sprint down and meet them at the studio. I was scared, really scared. What if they *do* go? But you just have to negotiate. In the end we just swapped the meal they weren't happy with for another one. I don't think their leaving was ever really on the cards.'

When you had the original idea did you think it would get this big?
'It was an idea that had been around for years. The original idea was for a group of celebrities to go on a walk, but it evolved into this. It's nice that it's a national obsession. The weird thing about it is that we're cut off from the reaction to it. By the time we get back to Britain it's all over. In a way it's good because we can get on with it without all the distractions. The press are very important, and it's great that they write about us, but it's got to the point where I don't even want to see the ratings. You just want to get on with making the programme without any distractions.'

Will there be a third series?
'That's up to Claudia Rosencrantz [ITV commissioning editor]. If there is a third series I'll be involved in some capacity, but maybe not this one. It's exhausting, working eighteen-hour shifts. Danniella's walking out one day and I think that the next day will be easier – and then we have a revolution on our hands! You never know what's going to happen next, but then that's probably what people like about it.'

Day Fourteen

When Ant and Dec announced that it was Antony's turn to take the long walk on Day Fourteen, it would've been fitting if Phil, Wayne, Fash and Linda had all stood up saying, "I'm Wozza!" "No, *I'm* Wozza!"

Sadly, it didn't happen. The great rebel leader gave himself up without a fight and the 'terrible trio' was broken. As always when someone leaves, the rest of them mourn for about half a second and then get on with it. Back in the studio with Ant and Dec, Antony looks thinner and wiser than when he went in. He says that he's learned a lot – and you can almost believe him.

How did they do?

ANTONY WORRALL THOMPSON: EVICTED – FIFTH

With his hangdog expression and boyish tufts of blonde

hair, Antony looks like Tintin – if the little Belgian had had a rough forty years after *The Calculus Affair*. Of all the celebs, he probably had the least to lose by going into the jungle: no one liked him very much before, and, now at least, everyone knows that he's got a few stories to tell. Which is convenient for someone with an auto-biography in 'all good bookshops' soon.

Highest high: Realizing that the celebs were much more powerful than they seemed and exploiting that by leading the great mutiny. He was the first person to understand the most important celebrity equation: no celebs = no show.

Lowest low: Walking into the trap on Day Thirteen. 'You did me like a kipper,' he had to admit, ruefully.

Best quote: 'F**k the calorific value!' (Surely appearing on an anti-dieting T-shirt near you soon.)

Entertainment value: 8/10. Great stories and a highly entertaining sense of mischief.

Niceness: 6/10. You could see why a lot of people don't like him, but he came out of it with his reputation very much enhanced.

When they leave the camp the celebs are whisked from an interview with Ant and Dec, into the waiting arms of their loved ones. Just behind their loved ones, though, hovers professional super-gooseberry Richard Squires. It's been his job to sooth the fraught nerves of the celebrities' partners for the past two weeks, and now it's his job to drag them away from the hotel Jacuzzi and into the equally loving arms of the press.

BEHIND THE LENS

Richard Squire: celebrity liaison

'It's almost harder for the celebrities' loved ones than it is for the celebrities. The partners have just been watching the programme for the last two weeks and they get very emotional and protective about certain storylines and about how they're portrayed.

'When they come out they just want to do everything at once. They want to go to Dreamworld, go paragliding, do everything they can – but of course they still have to do interviews. It's in their contract that they have to do one press, one TV and one Internet interview – but bringing the word 'contract' into a conversation is never a good idea!

'Danniella was offered a huge amount of money to sell her story, but she decided to do a press conference instead, because it wasn't about the money. She didn't want to be stalked by photographers. The day Toyah came out, people were following Chris and me into stores, paying shop assistants fifty to a hundred dollars to tell them what he'd bought!

'They are all disappointed to be voted out – it takes them until the next day when the next one's voted out to get over it. Then they realize that it's only one day that they lost! They all come out saying it's horrendous but they also say that it's changed them and they won't complain so much any more. Alana Stewart, from the American series, was in a restaurant telling us exactly that when her salad arrived and she said, 'This chicken's dry. I'm not eating that! Take it back!'

Meanwhile back in camp the remaining celebs have got one last day to try to persuade the public that they should be there at the death. Fash has discreetly picked up Catalina's trick: he's appearing with his shirt off at every opportunity now. Wayne has arranged one last camp (in every sense) dance. Linda is still striding the camp like Wonder Woman in gaiters. And cynical old Phil is still pulling the old 'What, is this a competition?' trick – the sly old devil.

They're all (with the possible exception of Phil) desperately trying to work out why the public keep voting for them so that they can play on it as much as possible. Fash, in particular, has been on a roller-coaster ride. Even though he claimed to believe that the public kept voting for him to take Bush Tucker trials because they wanted to see him doing his all-conquering action-hero thing, not even he really believed it.

But the fact that he's made it to the last four has given added credence to that view. If the public want action, thinks Fash, I'll give them action. Yesterday he promised to provide the 'best exercise regime seen so far'. He starts by hanging from a tree by his knees and trying to do sit-ups, only to be hindered by Wayne, who thinks he's stuck.

'Shall I give you a boost!' Wayne giggles.

'I don't need a boost!' says Fash with a lofty air, or the most lofty air you can muster when hanging from a tree by your knees.

Then, even worse, he tries to carry out a tricky yoga move known as 'the tree' (is that what you call them – yoga stance? yoga trick?) and topples slowly over. Poor

Fash probably thinks he's just blown his chances when, in fact, that mixture of ludicrous dignity is why he's still there on Day Fourteen. If there were to be a spin-off series from *I'm A Celebrity ...*, it would have to be *The Fash and Wayne Show*. Their double act took a little while to get going but by now it's one of the highlights.

But, when it comes down to it, it's every man (or woman) for himself (or herself), and Fash greedily takes on another Bush Tucker trial. Wayne has still got a bad leg from his trampolining accident (sorry, Wayne: it was from when you ... um, what was the story again?). But they all know that the trials are a great way to shine in the eyes of the public.

By now Fash has been through so many terrible experiences that he must think that he's survived the worst they could possibly throw at him. But he's wrong.

'What do you think "Eel Helmet" means?' Voice-y asks him in the Bush Telegraph. A brief flicker of trepidation crosses his normally impassive face.

'I think it means I should run,' he says, correctly.

One of the great things about the series has been the way that the celebrities accept the most ridiculous situations as a normal part of their daily life. No one will ever forget the sight of Wayne with waffles tied to his head, but Fash having freezing cold water and eels poured on his head must come close.

'The water must have to be so cold because it calms the eels down,' Fash rationalizes afterwards, endearingly crediting the trial organizers with a little more humanity than they deserve.

Of all the trials, this is the one that Fash would have liked to walk out on, but his old-fashioned side wouldn't let him. Linda got all the stars the day before and the mighty Fash wasn't going to be outdone by a girl.

With eels lazily wrapping themselves around his face, it's hard to see his expression when he's in there. Only the slow uncurling of his hands in calming tai chi moves (punches? tricks?) betrays his inner turmoil. When he gets out he looks shattered. Even Ant and Dec are alarmed when Dr Bob hurries over to administer oxygen, but Fash is fine and he stumbles back to camp triumphant once again.

The other partnership, Linda and Phil, is also stronger than ever. The pair are pretty close when sober, but with the addition of alcohol they've become expert at walking that thin line where friendship ends and something more than friendship begins.

'I love you,' Linda sighs, gazing into Phil's eyes.

'I love you, too,' says Phil, quickly adding, 'I love everyone.'

But their shared success in getting this far has brought all of the last four closer together. Even Wayne and Phil have managed to bury the hatchet – or at least chucked a thin covering of soil over it. Wayne is in a much better mood today as he gets a chance to lead them in an incredibly enthusiastic and happy series of dance moves. Before the series started, who would've thought that Fash could relax enough to join in something like that, or Phil summon up the energy?

With the euphoria still blazing away, Linda decides

that she wants to bring Fash and Wayne into her and Phil's love-in. With Fash, she succeeds almost immediately. 'I really love you, actually,' she tells Fash, repeatedly. (Did I mention they'd had a couple of bottles of wine?) 'I didn't like you at all to start with.'

'Oh, no, Lindy, no,' says Phil, shocked.

'It's not that I didn't like you,' Linda amends. 'But I didn't see anything to like. There wasn't anything between us.'

'But if there's nothing the first initial aspect should be to like, 'cos there's nothing to dislike,' says Phil slowly, like a slightly befuddled Jesus.

The others pause to consider this point, and then decide to go to bed – but Voice-y won't let them, realizing that there's more good stuff to come. 'Can the camp not go to bed yet?' she commands.

They sit back down and the conversation turns to who, if anyone, is playing to the cameras. Wayne is still convinced that Phil is, and this is the point at which, in another bizarre moment, they suddenly seem to be doing an unintentional *Goodfellas* pastiche with Wayne as Ray Liotta and Phil as Joe Pesci.

'I just think he's a natural performer,' Wayne shrugs awkwardly, unable to understand why Phil and Linda think this is a bad thing. 'He cracks me up. He's a natural entertainer.'

'I'm not,' says Phil, sensing some kind of implicit criticism. (You think I'm a comedian? You think I'm put on this earth to amuse you?)

'I don't think he's performing at all,' says Linda loyally.

There's an another awkward pause, but then, as so often before, they smooth it over and carry on.

Quote of the day

'I thought the Bush Tucker trials would be more of a physical thing: climb up a rope here, climb up a tree there, machine guns there.' Machine guns, Fash?

Tara Palmer-Tompkinson

How's it been on the other side of the camp wall?

'It's been the best job of my life. From doing it last year, I saw how much fun the crew had, and when they offered it to me I didn't hesitate. There are amazing energy levels. To do a couple of hours of live TV every day is just incredible. Everyone's working different shifts. It's quite comforting in a way – you know that, whatever time you come in, there are still people working. You don't have to worry about waking people up! I go to bed at four o'clock in the afternoon and get up at two so at least I won't have to worry about the time difference when I get back.'

You prefer this to last year?

'Definitely! I'd never go back for all the tea in China. I know at home people always ask whether there are secret treats or whatever, but there is nothing. It's really tough. It's tough to be deprived of all the things that you're used to. The food's really bland – it makes you appreciate the simple things in life like salt and pepper.'

But you were quite scathing about the rebellion over food?

'The rebellion was terrible. If you go into something, and say you're going to do it, especially if it's for charity, then you should do it. I thought of leaving at one stage but that's because it had seriously turned into *Lord of the Flies*. People really turned on me and that made me take a look at myself. When eight people don't like you, you know that you're doing something wrong. But when I sign on the line I sign with a lot of loyalty – not to leave, not to slag the show off. We were all so hungry. Your heart sinks when the basket comes down and you see how little it is, but we all used to think, Imagine the people with nothing, who have to live on less than this every day.'

Has what you learned last time stayed with you?

'Absolutely. I went in there and I was terrified of everything, but I overcame that and it made me stronger. It was a totally empowering experience. For the first time since I'd got over my addiction, I started having some respect for myself.'

Do you think anyone this time will have got as much out of it?

'Linda's really strong – although I think her voice is getting a bit annoying!'

The press said you had a 'catfight' with Catalina …

'There was no catfight. She felt that I should've

supported her, but I just think she should have taken a look at herself and learned something from being in there. But then no one said anything to her face – that was what was different this time. I believe that confrontation can only make relationships deeper in the long run.'

Is there anything they did that you thought, I wish we'd done that?

'Having ten cigarettes a day! Being a smoker, you know that, if someone annoys you, you can go and sit down on a rock and have a cigarette and that will calm you down. It seemed a little ironic that they didn't have food but they had cigarettes, but I can understand why the producers did it. They didn't want cigarettes to become an issue like they were last time.'

You 'tried' all the trials – or at least looked at them. What did you think?

'The trials were so tough this time. I'm amazed that they did them so well. The Eel Helmet was horrible but I'd have been able to do it. It's just a question of psyching yourself up. The one where Fash put his head in all the insects was the worst.'

Chris's guide to the trials: Part IV

TRIAL THIRTEEN: WHEEL OF HORROR

Contestant: Linda

'She got me again! She had a rat in her pants and it didn't even faze her. I'd love to have seen her with the eels because they're really hard to handle and she doesn't like them, but there wouldn't be much point fixing the wheel. If we really wanted to make her carry eels in her pants we could make that a compulsory part of the game!

'It would've been nice if there'd been an obstacle that gave her pause at least, but when you see her carrying a rat in her pants – and the rats were the point at where Fash refused to carry on in the first trial – what else can you do?'

TRIAL FOURTEEN: EEL HELMET

Contestant: Fash

'The dreaded Eel Helmet! I love that: it's just a really wild, bizarre idea. If you have some experience of snorkelling and you're not scared of eels, then it's pretty doable, but it is a really strange sensation. You can see what's going on outside but you're cut off by the water and the eels feel pretty strange rubbing against your face.

'Fash has given great trial all the way through. Fear of water? He's scared of everything! He got over all his fears in this one show! He was a little light-headed at the end. If you hyperventilate you can breathe too shallowly and end up with carbon dioxide in your blood, so that's why we have the oxygen standing by. He said afterwards that he's going to come looking for me in a dark alley!'

TRIAL FIFTEEN: BUSH TUCKER BONANZA (A.K.A. BALANCE)

Contestant: Phil

'Phil was great. I had no idea how he was going to respond but we tempted him with some pretty delicious stuff (the proper meals, not the Bush Tucker). We phoned Dawn and found out what his favourite meals were and there was Foster's beer and all this stuff he likes.

'The Bush Tucker was all stuff that Aborigines genuinely eat in the bush, but the part that gets left out is that they generally cook it. They wouldn't eat it as a snack like that, either, unless they were really hungry. It would be part of a meal. The ants are pretty nice: they have citric acid in and they're just like little bits of lime.'

TRIAL SIXTEEN: THE EEL TRANSFER (A.K.A. DETERMINATION)

Contestant: Linda

'Once again, Linda, always a competitor. We gave her a hint to catch them gently and she took that on board. The first one she tried to grab it and it took her about thirty seconds, but after that she went nice and slowly.

'If you grab them they pull away, but if you're nice and gentle they come with you. Eels was the one thing she said she didn't like on the Wheel of Horror, but give her credit: she did it.'

TRIAL SEVENTEEN: THE LOG ROLL (A.K.A. REACH)

Contestant: Fash

'This was a fun one. It's active, it's silly, you're going to fall off and end up in the water. Fash had a stroke of luck when he grabbed one, and another fell down, too, but he did really well.

'Again, he conquered water – we offered him a life vest but he turned it down. Fash is a great conman in the best possible way. I could tell they were all happy to have their last trial behind them. Seventeen trials in fifteen days – that's a lot for them and it's a lot for the crew.'

Insects have feelings too, you know ...

After witnessing the torture thousands of insects had to go through on Day Six, when they were poured over a sticky Danniella, getting trapped in her 'bristols', certain kind-hearted souls – notably Chris Packham of *The Really Wild Show*, um ... fame – were driven to protest. This is Chris Lore's response.

'We had the RSPCA on site every time we used animals, and they told us, "Whenever you use animals, even insects, people will complain." I understand where these people are coming from. The goal of the trials is not to hurt the animals. The critters are my best friends right now. I need them!

'I'm sure we lost some insects but not that many. We used most of them more than once! All those critters are bred to feed snakes, so I just feel like we're giving them a few more days in luxury. We look after them! They get to hang out, meet the celebs. I sleep at night!'

Jenni Falconer
I'm A Celebrity … Get Me Out Of Here! presenter
for GMTV

' I thought Danniella was going to win, to start with. She was getting all the press coverage in the beginning and she'd got this scoop with the story of her drug problems and how she overcame them. I thought the public would warm to her because of that.

'After she walked out I thought Phil was going to win, but we were hoping that Linda would win because men always win these reality shows! Also, I did wonder if the people who'd most like Phil would be students who'd need some kind of prize to vote! Or people who'd be too cool to vote.

'We've interviewed quite a few of the celebrities and they're all so glad to be back in their six-star hotel. When they came out they were just blabbering away, not even in complete sentences, but now they're so relaxed. Most of them just went to bed when they got out, but Wayne immediately went to drink. He'd had about three bottles of wine by the time I talked to him.

He was the funniest interview we've ever done, all these quotes like, 'Three musketeers? I call them the three musty queers!'

'I'm interviewing Fash next, so I want to ask him about how he thinks people have seen him. All of the others have said that he thinks he's one of the nation's heroes, so I want to see what he thinks the papers and people were saying about him. I feel sorry for Fash because we spoke to Antony and he told us that Fash was suffering from a kind of post-trial stress – he had nightmares, shakes, sweats. He's the one who deserves to win now.'

Day Fifteen

The cut on Day Fifteen was probably the unkindest yet. The last three would all be there on the final day but the odd one out has to walk. They began the fortnight believing that they understood what it would take to stay in the jungle, but they've been totally confused by the capricious public's voting patterns. They know it could be any of them. For all their insistence that they don't care who wins, they're all – maybe even Phil – starting to sense that victory is in sight now.

'Thank you very much. Fine. Yeah. Fine. Good, lovely,' Wayne says rapidly, when he learns that it's his turn to go. 'I didn't really want to win,' he announces to Ant and Dec later, with the exquisite grasp of celebrity speak that we've seen from him all the way through.

How did they do?

WAYNE SLEEP: EVICTED — SIXTH

Of all the celebs, Wayne looked in the most need of some time to himself. He was very happy to perform when the time came, and the others loved that, but he didn't want them to get behind the performance. After Danniella had left, he found it difficult having no one else around with a similar sense of humour. In the end he was probably closest to Fash. In a funny way the Nigerian diplomat and the flamboyant dancer seemed slightly isolated from the others by their extreme Englishness. They were the only two who were desperate to maintain their dignity and hold something back.

Highest high: Organizing the dancing on his last night and moulding Fash, Phil and Linda into a very passable chorus line.

Lowest low: Injuring his foot in an undignified trampolining accident and having to keep a stiff upper lip in the face of the others' unconcealed amusement.

Best quote (while putting on his damp raincoat on the first day): 'I feel like a used condom.'

Entertainment value: 8/10. For one of the great TV moments, when he crawled through a tunnel of rats with waffles tied to his head, for some hilarious quips and for some surreal jungle dancing.

Niceness: 6/10. Held Danniella together for a few days, even if it was by sniping at the others.

And then there were three, as Fash says repeatedly throughout the day. By now practically every other word they say is a catchphrase or an in-joke of some kind. The always ubiquitous *'bubeleh'* (see Glossary) is now coming out every few seconds.

It's just as well that they don't have to spend the whole day talking to each other. According to people who've spoken to the celebs on the outside, they all speak in broken sentences when they come out and, given a few more days, it looks as if Fash, Phil and Linda would be reduced to variations on 'bub-sy', 'it's all good in the hood' and 'bring it on'.

Luckily, the producers have kindly fixed up three last Bush Tucker trials for them to be getting on with. In one final, cruel trick they even give the trials code names and make the celebs choose their own from: 'Balance', 'Reach' and 'Determination'.

'I've got pretty good balance,' muses Phil, probably imagining he'll have to do some kind of tightrope walk over a pool of plastic crocodiles. He should know it's not that simple, though, when Voice-y instructs him to 'dress to impress'. Maybe he just thinks his constant visits to the Bush Telegraph have paid off at last and he's scored.

Lucky he's got someone with a bit of fashion sense around to give him advice. 'You should wear your shorts – that'll impress the girls,' Linda instructs him. 'The hat's quite impressive, the gaiters are quite impressive and …' But she can't keep it up. 'Actually you look diabolical,' she admits.

With a handmade bowtie around his neck, Phil lopes down to the Trial Area to be confronted with nothing that looks as though it could be involved in a balancing act. Unless it's the table. He's undoubtedly made unsuccessful attempts to balance on a table before, and there is a pint of beer and a couple of cigarettes waiting for him, along with several plates of food. Maybe that's it.

'It *is* to do with balance,' says Ant disingenuously. 'A balanced diet. You can eat all of this any time you want' (he gestures towards platefuls of nice food) 'or you can eat this' (he gestures towards a covered plate).

'It's all good stuff, is it?' Phil asks nervously as Dec removes the cover to reveal a plate with a strange, brown lump on it. 'It's all edible?'

However cruel the producers are to them, the celebs still cling to the belief that there must be a heart there somewhere. They wouldn't make them do anything *that* bad.

That belief rapidly disappears for Phil as he cracks open the lump to expose a wriggling, squirming creature. They stare at each other in mutual disbelief for what seems like minutes before Phil finally, almost retching, swallows it whole and washes it down with a huge gulp of water.

'Shall we take a look at the next one?' asks Ant.

'Yeah,' says Phil, flatly.

'Probably best to chew this one,' Dec informs him as two little bugs squirm all over each other.

'Oh my God, they're getting it on,' cries Phil. He hesitates for even longer this time. Whether that is out of a romantic desire to let them say their last goodbyes, or because he's just seen that this one's got teeth, it's hard to tell. 'Have we got a bit of time for this one?'

'Yeah,' says Dec. 'Although we do have to be back in camp by tomorrow morning!'

After that it can only get easier. He downs everything else with barely a murmur, and Ant and Dec are so impressed that they even let him drink the beer. 'Cheers,' he says, quickly making away with the cigarettes before they can say anything.

Fash, who takes 'Reach', gets an easier trial for once, although it does involve yet another of his phobias: water. He has to walk out on a slippery, revolving beam above a small lake and grab the stars that are hanging from a rope above. Since the water's only waist deep, though, it doesn't look quite as terrifying for this confirmed hydrophobe as the Eel Helmet was. He makes it look pretty easy, anyway, even seeing off Chris Lore's mischievous suggestion that he could do the trial in just his swimming costume.

'Are there leeches in there?' he asks suspiciously. By now Fash knows not to be too trusting.

'There will be leeches,' Dr Bob admits. 'I think I'd keep the trousers on.'

Fash wins all five stars. By now the camp have got two full courses coming to them, prepared by the crew, and it's just Linda left, taking on 'Determination'.

That name's slightly disingenuous, too. 'Subtlety' would be a better one, or even 'Tricksiness'. The trial is officially called 'The Eel Transfer', but they knew that gutsy Linda would go for 'Determination' rather than 'Reach' or 'Balance' – and certainly rather than anything that mentioned eels. She's already told them that she hates them. 'Horrible creatures,' she squirms.

It's not even as if determination were much use in the trial. Linda may be determined to get the eels out of one tank and into another, but they're equally determined to stay exactly where they are. In the end she manages to catch them only with a more discreet, tickling motion. Eels, as Dr Bob reminds her, are fish, and not 'members of the snake family', as Fash claimed yesterday when trying to recruit them into one of his pre-existing phobias, rather than having to introduce yet another one (his phobia diary ran out of pages several days ago).

She gets four of the five stars, though. If they'd done that well all the way through then the Great Sausage Mutiny might never have happened. By now they're dealing with everything that gets thrown at them and Fash even makes a shocking admission. 'This has been a real holiday for me,' he says.

'I was a real wreck,' he admits, when asked why he wanted to come to the camp. 'I just wanted to get away from everyone.' One of the reasons he gives for joining the programme is the stress of having to pay employees, which will probably ring bells with a lot of people who are owed money by someone like Fash. The cheque isn't in the post. It's just that the person who owes you money is out sticking his head in a tray full of bugs in the jungle somewhere.

Quote of the day

'You know my phobias: water! It had to be, didn't it?' Well, no: it could've been almost anything, Fash

Day Sixteen:
The Final Eviction

By now it's hard to believe that it's only been two weeks. Our three remaining celebs have changed both at the most basic level, in that they look quite a bit thinner, but also they claim that they've changed on a deeper level, too becoming better, nicer people. Whether that's true we'll only see when they're faced with the temptation to throttle the 'friends' from last year who advised them to take part. (Wonder what Danniella's going to say to Nell McAndrew, or Fash to Nigel Benn?)

Actually it seems like they might be grateful to them. Once again most of the celebs have come out of the jungle smelling of roses (metaphorically at least. Anyone who attended the final eviction will tell you that roses were not the first thing that sprang to mind when confronted with three people who hadn't had access to a shower for two weeks.).

Phil says he's left baggage behind in there ('at least a few rucksacks' he specifies with his characteristic ability to squeeze metaphors till they burst); Antony says it was a life-changing experience; Catalina says that she's going to become more famous than any of them (hang on, I thought she said she didn't want. . .oh, never mind); Danniella said that it's helped her to realise what's important to her.

Either way, it doesn't seem like winning is the most important thing. When they're asked to make one final plea to the public even Fash looks slightly embarrassed. But they're all competitors and having come this far they'd all like to be crowned king, or queen.

'I can't say "don't vote for Linda, a mother, or Phil, a great guy,"' says Fash but you can see that he'd like his legions of Fash Fans to read between the lines.

'Vote for me,' says Linda, still managing to make naked ambition look charming and honest.

'I don't know why you should vote for me,' says Phil, but you can tell that he would like it if you could think of a few reasons.

One and a half million votes later and there's still only 250 votes in it. But Linda's family must wish that they'd dialed a few more times because she's the one who has to leave first.

How did they do?

LINDA BARKER: EVICTED SEVENTH (CAME THIRD)

Linda was a bit of a revelation. It's notoriously difficult for women to be ambitious and energetic without being seen as pushy and aggressive but she did it and managed to appeal to men and women. The constant making-over of the camp could have got annoying but the absence of Laurence Llewellyn Bowen made it just about bearable. And, surprisingly, she saw off Catalina and Danniella to become the number one pin-up of the series. Mark Durden-Smith was particularly keen.

Highest high: Hurling chunks of bee-hive at a startled Ant and Dec during the 'Terror In The Trees' trial.

Lowest low: Breaking down in tears when she received the letter from her husband, Chris.

Best quote: 'The guys have told me not to trust you,' breaking Ant and Dec's hearts.

Entertainment value: 7/10 As well as being consistently bubbly she's also got a place in history as one of Reality TV's great drunks' ('I really love you. . .I really, really love you.')

Niceness: 8/10 You can't fake the kind of sympathy that she showed towards Phil in his hour of need and she even brought Fash out of his shell in the last couple of days.

'That's a joke,' says Phil when he hears the result of the first vote, genuinely shocked that he and Fash have got more votes than the lovely Linda.

Fash is even more surprised. At last, today, he admits that his faith in the great British Public has been shaken over the two weeks. 'You weren't sure if the UK public was voting 'cos they wanted to see you, or 'cos they thought you were a crazy man,' he says of his record six Bush Tuckers.

It still doesn't occur to him that both might be true.

When it comes down to it, though, everyone knows that Phil has to be the winner.

'And the King Of The Jungle is …' teases Ant with a long pause. Phil manages to keep a straight face for about two seconds but by the time the result is announced he's already giggling at the ridiculous tension. It is, after all, just a game. And it took him a long time to admit even that.

Even Fash has to admit that the right man won.

How did they do?

JOHN FASHANU: EVICTED EIGHTH (CAME SECOND)

In years to come when people look back on this year's *I'm A Celebrity* ... it will be Fash they remember. With his numerous phobias (all heroically conquered), Herculean exercise regime and strict values he was a strange mixture of action man and Mary Poppins. Trials Supervisor Chris Lore will always love him for the way he made the Bush Tucker Trials look impossibly exciting and dangerous. Towards the end Fash even tried out a little humanity for size, opening up to Wayne and Linda.

Highest high: Too many to note but special mention should go to his daring escape from the 'Bridge Of Doom', and his courageous defeat of the 'Snake Pit'.

Lowest low: Everyone knows that Fash is a showman but his trauma after the horrendous 'Eel Helmet' wasn't faked.

Best quote: 'I don't even want to eat it. Just let me look at it and smell it. I want to take it to bed,' hunger does strange things to a man.

Entertainment value: 10/10 A great cult hero on so many different levels.

Niceness: 6/10 Who knows what's going on behind that mask, but Fash convinced the other celebs and they had to live with him for two weeks.

Meanwhile Phil still looks exactly the same as he did all that time ago when the (lucky?) carpet python crapped all over him. 'It's unbelievable,' he says. 'I only turned up for a kip for two weeks.'.

How did they do?

PHIL TUFNELL: KING OF THE JUNGLE

Even writing 'Phil Tufnell: King Of The Jungle' seems slightly ridiculous. If they'd given him a proper crown made out of gold, rather than just a few leaves, he'd still have lost it or swapped it for a packet of Benson and Hedges on the way out. He was favourite to win from the beginning because he was a character, but he won ultimately because he was a genuine person. One day, when Universities are doing degree courses in how to survive reality TV, he'll be a term on his own. Don't laugh. I bet the University Of High Wycombe are writing the curriculum now.

Highest high: Turning down the wine on his birthday, offering a camera operator £500 for five cigarettes, (I bet he still regrets the fact he turned it down), teaching the camp how to play cricket, too many others to mention.

Lowest low: Realising that Wayne didn't like him as much as he liked Wayne.

Best quote: 'I just want some ever'

Entertainment value: 10/10

Niceness 10/10

Quote of the day

(from Linda's husband Chris Short) 'It's like watching rats in a laboratory, but you happen to be married to one of the rats.'

Quote of the series

'I had a great time mate, thanks for inviting me.' Phil puts the boot into the broken-hearted producers.

Bring on next year …

Glossary

Big 'un: Fash or Antony.

Bubeleh (pronounced *bob-a-lah*): Yiddish term of endearment introduced to the camp by Fash, often accompanied by waggling one's hands above one's head as though wearing comedy antlers.

Bub-sy (pronounced bob-sy): Affectionate derivative of *bubeleh*.

Cadbury Girl: See Voice-y.

The Cat: Phil Tufnell.

Changing your shoes: evacuating your bowels.

Going out for lunch: Doing a Trial or going out to get the celebrity chest (particularly used by Linda, and accompanied by happy jumping up and down as in 'We're going out for lunch!').

I want out: 'Please vote for me, please!' or 'I want out!'

It's all disco: See *It's all good in the hood*.

It's all good in the hood: Things are going as well as can be expected.

It's all good in the wood: See *It's all good in the hood*.

Kitty Kat: Fash and Phil's name for Catalina.

Lazy disease: Affliction (discovered by Fash) that threatens those who don't carry sacks of rocks around with them at all times.

Lovely: Linda's name for Phil and, latterly, Fash. Also Phil's name for Linda.

Pretty tea: A particularly nice version of *Ugli tea* (see below).

Sleep-o: Wayne.

Tommo: Antony Worrall Thompson.

Tomorrow's a good day to die: Tomorrow would be a good day to be evicted (used by Fash every day after evictions started).

Toy: Toyah.

Ugli tea: Faux tea usually made from the skin of the Ugli fruit, but also at times from other bits of fruit they've got lying around.

Voice-y: Bush Telegraph voice and source of torrid fantasy for Phil.

Wayne's World!: Cried à la the film of that name, when Wayne does something odd.

Well done, Neddy!: Fash's words of encouragement for Wayne.

Westy: Danniella Westbrook.

Wozza: Antony Worrall Thompson.

Y: Australian-style addition to names by Phil: e.g. Sian-y, Lind-y etc.